BODY HIGH

BODY HIGH

Death, Drugs, and Eva Hesse

Ryann Donnelly

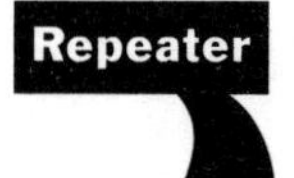

Published by Repeater Books

An imprint of Watkins Media Ltd

Unit 11 Shepperton House

89–93 Shepperton Road

London

N1 3DF

United Kingdom

www.repeaterbooks.com

A Repeater Books paperback original 2025

1

Distributed in the United States by Random House, Inc., New York.

ISBN: 9781915672872

Ebook ISBN: 9781915672889

The manufacturer's authorised representative in the EU for product safety is

eucomply OÜ - Pärnu mnt 139b-14, 11317 Tallinn, Estonia, hello@eucompliancepartner.com,www.eucompliancepartner.com

Printed and bound by CPI Group (UK) Ltd, Croydon, CR0 4YY

For my Auntie Kate and Marcus, who took me to the very important exhibition where these ideas first began to take shape. And to Tariq, who agreed to put out a book about them. xoxo

Absolute 0

The dead body of my boyfriend's younger brother, Eric, is in a cardboard coffin which I can see from the backseat of a black sedan following the hearse. Printed on the coffin's high-gloss, ultra-white surface are images that have been gently distorted from being enlarged for this format: poorly lit phone pictures of the deceased with his cat and cherry-red clipart guitars that cross at their necks with little lightning bolts around the headstocks are among the elements of this most absolutely fucked up collage. The selection was curated by his mother, who I deign to guess was going for "sensitive young man… my favorite… had a guitar just like this." But this coffin is giving: thirty-seven-year-old burnout enabled by infantilizing mum. It's giving: It's better this way.

The coffin is removed from the hearse and hoisted onto the shoulders of male family members and Eric's friend Richard, whose grief is palpable. A cold, thick haar attends him, which I consciously decide I can't be near. The coffin edge digs into his trapezius muscle, and the physical and probably psychic weight bend him into a crescent shape as he enters the crematorium in Cornwall. It's as quaint as such a place can be: small white chapel in front, retort in back, and surrounded by grass knolls rendered a garish electric green in the sun. It's a new cemetery, dotted with less than a dozen headstones, offering the illusion that death is sort of out of fashion. It's July. Hot. Glistening sweat collects around hairlines in marquise and pear shapes like bad engagement-ring stones, and I worry about the thickness of the coffin's corrugated stock and how well they prepare bodies that are just going to be cremated anyway. I wonder how they keep one person's ashes from mixing with someone else's and resolve that they probably don't. Party.

I'm considering gross logistics because I don't have any sadness left for this occasion. All my sadness — let's say about forty metric tons, enough to fill all the as yet undug graves across the tastelessly vital lawn which frames this scene — has already been committed to other dead or dying things. My boyfriend, Nathan, suffers the same disease of addiction which has just killed his brother, and it has feasted on our lives this year. My money and his body fat were its appetizers, our hopes and dreams its rich mains. We tried to hide from it in beautiful places, but it was always there. Things were stolen, cars were smashed up, and there was even a baptism. I feel heavier and slower every day, and I'm not speaking much. All I have the will to hope for is that his mother doesn't put pictures of us on his coffin.

Death is a demon triplet which possesses me in rotation: fear, expectation, denial. The distinct consciousness that I feel when one of them is inside me is always directed onto the same subject. I watch him, and I watch him, and I watch him.

(I want your soul, I will eat your soul…
Come to daddy… Come to mummy…)

Technology

I tried a variety of therapeutic strategies to deal with these events, both as they were happening and in the years after they occurred: painting, pedicures, actual therapy. What helped to remedy the grief I felt for my doomed relationship with an addict, and all the energy I wasted trying to save it, was standing in front of rather hideous sculptures. Things like Eva Hesse's *Untitled (Seven Poles)* (1970), Alina Szapocznikow's *Stèle* (1968), and others I'll discuss in this book lulled and soothed. To some extent this was an unsurprising cure. I'm a singer and an art historian; making and viewing art in a variety of media has always given me pleasure. But these objects had never appealed to me in this way before. It was bittersweet. Historically, I was interested in the kind of sexually provocative, shocking performance and video work that made me feel emboldened and vital and — trite as it is — alive. Carolee Schneemann, Yoko Ono, Ana Mendieta. They didn't work like that anymore. I no longer felt young, or hot, or my own, and they reminded me of this. The sculptures I was drawn to were, instead, tender and morbid: dead alive. They dripped, collapsed, caved, stretched, and some looked like they'd been covered in spit and tears. They gave shape to the hideous feelings I grappled to understand or describe until I encountered them. Having them in front of me also offered the illusion that they had been removed from my body — even if only for the minutes I spent in their company. They made me feel light and medicated: a body high.

With further research, I found that these works had all been made by women who were dealing with comparably challenging experiences related to physical and mental health. Their works have commonly been read as representations of their own bodies in the throes of these significant events. Hesse's exploration of ephemerality through skin-like resins and weathered plastics has been linked to her diagnosis with the brain tumor that killed her. Szapocznikow represented her cancer as hot-pink resin breasts that appeared to melt. What I think has been missed in the scholarship on these artists, though, is how their practices also functioned as an effective method of care. Creating these works allowed the artists to externalize parts of their body that could be tended to and re-imagined. The direct touching, shaping, and assembly of their forms resonated with common care practices, from holding hands to dressing wounds. These processes put them in positions of care, which, I argue, also provided a therapeutic effect. Given the severity of Hesse's and Szapocznikow's illnesses, I cannot imagine they would have continued making their work until their deaths if it had made them feel *worse*.

I do not think it is a coincidence that the remedial effect I experienced in front of these objects was also likely to have been sought by the artists making them. I do think that the events of the last several years have increased the pursuit of, need for, and interest in care, which have made these insights — and my attraction to this particular group of works in the first place — a product of their time. My experience living in proximity to addiction from 2015–16, near the peak of the opioid crisis, was hardly unique. From 2013 to 2019, in the United States alone, the synthetic opioid death rate increased by 1040 percent (so we're clear, that's not a typo: one thousand and forty percent).[1] The physical and emotional recovery which these events necessitated for so many would be intensified and complicated by the COVID-19 pandemic. Resources were exhausted. We were isolated. It also does not escape me that the grief and loss delivered by these medical crises were only compounded by systemic racism, which, as it revealed itself in myriad forms — from the toxic rhetoric of a racist president, to police brutality caught on tape, and disproportionate COVID deaths among people of color — required a need for increased anti-racism work. This included protesting en masse at a time when it had never been more dangerous to do so, and in spite of the fact that energy reserves were bone dry. We were thrust into a relationship of unprecedented intimacy with illness and treatment, on a previously unknown scale. Most people lacked a clear understanding of how to engage with this new terrain, something this book hopes to remedy.

The opioid crisis and pandemic informed how I developed my research on these works. This book explores these strange, gorgeous artworks, and the things that led the artists who made them — and me — to seek their therapeutic effects. It developed out of the simple desire to make you feel the same deep, dark catharsis I felt in front of those sculptures, which I know might seem niche, or just so, so small. But we know the feeling of medicating ourselves, and the frustration of not being able to cure the people we love. These works and experiences offer models for care that are simple and which resonate with the collective need to recover.

To achieve this, the book moves between autobiography and the visual analysis which was informed by it. Increasingly, this method has been captured by the term "autotheory" and has feminist aims which chime with those of the artworks explored in this book. Lauren Fournier, author of the text *Autotheory as Feminist Practice in Art, Writing, and Criticism*

(2021), offers a definition of the field, which I think is worth quoting here at length for how it summarizes the aim of this book's approach and structure:

> Autotheory is a term that describes contemporary works of literature, art, and art writing that integrates autobiography and other explicitly subjective and embodied modes with discourses of philosophy and theory in ways that transgress genre conventions and disciplinary boundaries.[2]

What is important here is that the mix of personal and philosophical writing described above offers transgressive potential, and also that visual art might have the capacity to function as both a mode of life-writing and as theoretical text. Referring back to the classic feminist assertion that "the personal is political," Fournier resolves that the history of feminism is, in a sense, a history of Autotheory.[3] For her, theorizing through lived experience is a feminist approach. This has greatly informed the approach of this book, and the appraisal of the objects it considers as feminist. I consider the autobiographical artworks I will explore here as a form of feminist autotheory, and the autotheoretical writing about them as a comparable artistic practice.

There are further implications in her description of autotheory as a "subversive or transformative mode of critiquing institutional powers."[4] As a critique of institutional power, the method attempts to deconstruct, or simply bring into view and put pressure on, a hierarchical organization of knowledge and research methods which has, until recently, degraded the use of the personal and creative as evidential. An autotheoretical approach supports the idea that some (most) voices and experiences have been considered of lesser value than those which have historically informed more conventional theoretical frameworks, and that drawing on a wider range of lived experiences benefits discourse.

This is not an uncommon approach, particularly for art historical texts. Curator Legacy Russell's *Glitch Manifesto* (2020) explores her experience of online communities and identity-making to consider new iterations of digital feminism, and *Time is the Thing a Body Moves Through* (2023) by T. Fleischmann is a personal favorite for its use of the art of Félix González-Torres as a thematic compass for navigating the body, loss, and sexuality. Perhaps most well-known is Maggie Nelson's memoir *The Argonauts* (2015), which uses autobiography in her readings of scholars like Ludwig Wittgenstein and Judith Butler to explore queer love and family life.[5] There's Paul B. Preciado's *Testo Junkie* (2008), Christina Sharpe's *Ordinary Notes* (2023), the list goes on… In these texts, personal experiences form critical lenses through which the authors explore new perspectives and insights.

This book extends the feminist aims of the examples and structures described above through its more explicit exploration of *care* as part of its autotheoretical approach. Specifically, this book explores what I will refer to as "creative feminist care," defined here as therapeutic yet under-appreciated practices performed outside institutions.[6] While thinking of care in this way continues the exploration of institutional critique introduced above, this book should not be considered skeptical of the medical or scientific. However, it does acknowledge the tensions between the agency and benefits provided by more conventional modes of care, and the control levelled over the body by medical institutions, historically organized within a patriarchal framework. Further, this exploration of care outside institutions does not promote the idea that care should be an individual endeavor. In their *Care Manifesto* (2020), the UK's Care Collective emphasizes that "care is also a social capacity… to put care centre stage means recognising and embracing our *interdependencies*."[7]

This book pursues a model of autobiography explored by theorist Michel Foucault, which resonates deeply with the artists' apparent need for care indicated by their own autobiographical approaches, and indeed a desire to treat and re-define their bodies through extra-institutional practices. In his text *Technologies of the Self* (1988), Foucault considers how the process of knowing one's self relies on caring for one's self. "In Greek and Roman texts," he says, "the injunction of having to know yourself was always associated with the other principle of having to take care of yourself… knowledge of oneself appeared as a consequence of taking care of yourself."[8] Foucault describes the self in these contexts as more a soul than a body, but explains that care was still carried out in non-abstract, essentially physical and tangible ways, through a "network of obligations and services."[9] He explains that writing was also important to the culture of taking care of one's self, and that one of the main features of taking care involved "taking notes on one's self to be re-read… and keeping notebooks in order to reactivate for one's self the truths one needed… taking care of one's self became linked to constant writing activity."[10] Foucault identified this as a key way humans developed knowledge of themselves.

This book enacts this methodology: writing the self to care for the self, but also to produce and apply knowledge. In this case, that knowledge is applied to the very objects which catalyzed an awareness of the need for care. I would not have been able to provide you with the knowledge I have of these works had they not first had the intense therapeutic effect on me that they did. The feelings they gave me made me want to know more about them. The book doesn't only endeavor to be personally curative, but to extend care in the same way the sculptural objects, which grappled with the lives of the artists who made them, had a therapeutic impact on me when I encountered them. The autobiographical parts of this book, I hope, will resonate with those who have had similar experiences, or who are in comparable situations. But the text also attests to the value of others' autobiographies. I needed the artwork discussed in this book in order to understand and confront the experiences they seemed to reify and corroborate. This book argues against the common critique of autobiography as indulgent and limited. It receives and responds to autobiography as reciprocal practice. Its aims are discursive and reparatory, rather than didactic and terminal. It models one of the methods of care it promotes and observes in the works it describes. Given Foucault's penchant for focusing on the lives of men, the use of this particular "technology" should also be seen as appropriative.

Lastly, the use of autobiography here offers an art history that is personal and lived through. I know discussions of AI have become ubiquitous, and I was hesitant to include any mention of it here. It gives me the ick. It's gauche. But this text responds to my fears of AI stripping my discipline, my remedy, of so much of its vibrancy and grit. In 2023, my students' use of AI became utterly apparent. The result was writing that lacked the sense of an embodied experience of the work it described — lacking verve, lacking a reckoning with art's emotional capacity and value. It felt like they'd stopped looking. What even are we doing at that point? I recognize that I'm drawing on one limited body of evidence. But I fear this gutless, impersonal analysis becoming commonplace, or worse, our relying on AI to translate our most visceral, vital feelings for us because it saves time, because we're exhausted. This book let me revisit and examine the experiences that led me to see these works the way I do. Through this process I have become my own again, and try to offer some new ideas about Hesse and others. A lot of it's ugly and not much fun, but I imagine Hesse felt the same way about *Seven Poles* (1970). So here's what happened.

Cyclops, or, The Beginning

I hold dear the memory I have of your hands surrounding my face, and the force and speed with which you drew our mouths together. I remember a glimpse of your left hand moving so quickly from your side to touch me that your fingers blurred. Your hand stretched so wide that your index finger rested against the underside of my earlobe and pressed into that soft skin. Your thumb brushed against the corner of my eye, where my top and bottom eyelashes met, and everything got so slow and perfect that it felt like every lash bent gently back against the coarse minutia of your fingerprint, like pressing back the teeth of a comb, one by one. Plink-plink, plink. I could, and can now, feel your little finger, angled down on my throat, and the thinnest edges of fingernails run through my hair along my scalp. The cold made our breath visible, and when our lips parted, our exhalations clouded around a strand of saliva thinner than spider silk that snapped as we came back into each other's focus.

You had two very good tricks.

Trick one:

It is best if one person is laying down on their back in a bed. The other person should kneel next to them, lean over them, and align their face to the person's beneath them. Do not kiss, but touch lips. The person laying down should look to their left at the same time that the person above looks to their right. Your heads should be facing the same direction, and your lips should now only be connected at the edges. Slowly turn your head in the opposite direction, then back. Repeat. Your lips should connect like a little franking machine.

Trick two:

Your nose and the nose of the person you want to love you must touch. Tilt your head forward so that your foreheads touch too — a pyramid shape. Smush together as close as possible without becoming uncomfortable. Look straight at each other until your focus softens and the other person becomes a cyclops.

"I've fallen for the Cyclops," I told my friends.

You sent me a *New York Times* article about a study in which some psychologists tried to make strangers fall in love with each other; they wanted to see if love could be produced at will. Pairs were given a long questionnaire, then they had to stare at each other for three minutes. *The Times* published the questions, and we tried to get through them but only answered six. You got cagey and we kissed instead.

Informing me that you lived in a rehabilitation center for drug addicts, alcoholics, and compulsive gamblers was your way of telling me that you could no longer hold my face in your hands, or lay invisible postage marks across my lips, or call me. There was a short series of rejections to my invitations to see and do things, but not before I took the knowledge of where you lived and why with me from England to Seattle to New York and back to England. In that two-week period, I lived with this information comfortably. I had gone back home to Seattle to play a show and do an art exhibition called *Homme Sick*. Fitting. I wish you could have seen it. While I was there, I saw an Ann Hamilton retrospective at Seattle's Henry Art Gallery, where visitors were invited to tear sheets from pads of paper nailed to the wall that were printed with the bodies of animals that were not only dead, but twisted, flattened, decayed, and generally wrong looking. I sent some to you in the mail.

I would like to think that you fell for me accidentally, hard, and made the rational decision to focus on your recovery rather than me. Even if this was the case, I don't know that you would have been able to identify it in such a way. I think your body just moved and that you didn't feel it necessary to explain these instincts in words. Maybe you just didn't feel what I felt.

No Fury Like

I rolled around heartbroken for a couple weeks and tried to take my revenge by making something. He was an artist. He had done graffiti for years, then had unexpected success in the wake of Banksymania after something of his went into Phillips' contemporary auction as "Street Art." But this wasn't a lucky break. He was excellent. Sometimes the best way to get an artist to love you is to make art that's more beautiful than theirs. I tried to use references to our brief time together — films we'd seen, books we'd read — subversive codes that would say: I could have handled it. I could have held you. You're never gonna find another girl who loves all this weird shit like I do.

I had moved to London from New York to do a PhD, and was making music and videos as part of the practice-based degree. This was a new iteration of my background as the singer of a thrashy but danceable punk band I'd been in for a decade. I was playing shows, freelancing for a magazine, and filming things to be used as projections during live sets with the new friends I'd made in the eighteen months I'd been in London. These films consisted mostly of slow-motion vignettes whose value and intrigue I located in the uncertainty surrounding the physical and romantic relationship between the performers. Amy and I passed an oyster back and forth between our mouths under red light. I unbuttoned Gianpaolo's dress shirt as Gianpaolo unbuttoned my dress shirt and we slowly re-dressed each other, both looking down at gently touching, busy hands. Ayo, Nadine, Elise, Anna, Michelle, and I lay on the ground, filmed from above, and made small, coordinated movements until we ended up in a massive body heap, limbs tangled and draped, quite intentionally somewhere between an orgy and a mass grave. I tattooed a Matisse drawing on Amy's inner thigh — one we'd seen together at the chapel he designed in Vence, France. None of it was revelatory, but it was tender and simple, and it did what it set out to, which was to offer new iterations of intimate, if not sexual, relationships. Being in them was fine, but I loved making them more. Even if the Cyclops would never see these things, they assured me he had made a mistake.

I proceeded to meet the nicest, dullest boy: a graphic designer with limited creativity. He was good at branding things like bottled water and house paint. He introduced me to his nice parents after three weeks. He paid for dinners. My exit came sooner than it might have were he not the worst lover I have ever known. There's an episode of *Sex and the City* in which Carrie can't walk upright at Charlotte's wedding because she's been fucked by a menace whose fuck moves she compares to those of a jackrabbit. Watch that ep on fast forward and you'll get a version closer to what I was dealing with. I asked him about it, and he said it was "just what he needed to get where he was goin'." Hm. How to argue with one's needs… Realizing I could not possibly have sex with him one more time, but also that nothing he said, ever, made me laugh, challenged me, or introduced some way of seeing a film or hearing a piece of music that was even a little bit interesting, I opened Tinder and began looking for someone else who might do at least one of those things. Instead, what I found was an opportunity to regain proximity to the Cyclops, and I acted on it. If this had not resulted in the bad things, then I would have qualified my behavior as immature, fun. Perhaps it's because of what followed that I see this decision as so horribly vain: me at my very worst.

Asking for it

On Tinder you used to be able to see if you had mutual friends with people you might date. I swiped right when I came across an attractive man whose profile showed the Cyclops in the shared friends area. In his black-and-white portrait, cropped at the shoulders, he looked forward, expressionless but commanding. He wore the kind of thick, dark-rimmed glasses that make everyone look a little extra bold, and thus hot, and a white button-up shirt. He looked polished, serious, but like an artist, not a businessman. He described himself as a photographer. Nathan (Death). He was a kind of Death that was everywhere all the time rather than a single grim-reaper figure — stale cola, dust, the slow fadeout of Fleetwood Mac's masterpiece, "The Chain," but sure, also catastrophic loss of life. I think Nathan was mostly Death, and the very classically dark kind. He carried it like syphilis — a slowly progressing and degenerative disease which could be transmitted through fucking, but let's say in this case, also love. I caught Death from Nathan.

For our first date, we arranged to meet at the pagoda in Victoria Park. When I arrived, he was facing away from the entrance, looking at the water through the other open doorway in the structure. I went to tap his shoulder. I got close to him, but he turned around before I could reach him. I have now marked, on the barely perceptible air displaced by his turning body, my feelings of distrust, mistake, and fear. At the time, perhaps these were the feelings of having been caught.

I inhaled quickly and stepped back, like when gymnasts come off the vault with too much force.

We sat by the pond in front of the pagoda in a patch of grass notably less kempt than some of the surrounding areas, which were more obviously designated for lying around on blankets, being visible. It was sunny, but I suffered a cool breeze in a sleeveless vintage co-ord skirt set with little roses all over it. I wore my brown hair up with bangs swept aside. I was trying to grow them out. He had dirty-blond hair and blue eyes. Chiseled features. Tall and thin. I never thought we looked right together. Amy astutely pointed out when she met him that he looked like the actor Richard E. Grant when he was young. He even sounded like him, actually. About ten minutes into this date, he leaned in to kiss me as I was mid-sentence. I hadn't felt it coming, and it didn't really make any sense. Every other time I'd been first-kissed, there had been a more noticeable lead-up. I felt the dispossession of being interrupted, the arrest of a physical invasion, but also some power, like I had made him want me uncontrollably.

He went home that night, but we got through the love questionnaire the next morning over coffee in bed.

When I start seeing someone, I try to get them into a museum, gallery, or, ideally, a weird performance art thing as soon as possible. It feels the same as introducing them to my friends. It shows me whether they can be vulnerable, if they're curious and imaginative, whether they have a sense of humor, and whether I might one day be able to live with this person's preferred aesthetic in a domestic arena: What will they put on the walls? What might our silverware look like? Can they handle my collection of framed Félix González-Torres posters, which amount to seven variations of nearly, but not quite, blank pieces of big white paper? It is more important for me to figure out this latter point than it is to know whether they have a savings account or how often they shower. Call it superficial and you're missing the point of this book, which is that art can often be the crucial medium through which the raw material of pleasure and pain become thoughts and ideas to be exchanged.

To stress this point: the very nice boy I dated just before I met Nathan kept trying to see stuff in the Jackson Pollocks that we saw at the Royal Academy's Abstract Expressionism show. He saw nice things: a cow, a cat, clouds. He made everything nicer, like him. This was fine — lovely in fact — but it suggested to me that he was afraid, or simply unable, to feel the slashes and gashes and storms of fervent gestures that Pollock laid upon blank space until there was none, precisely in his refusal to paint "stuff" which could be seen out the window or in the thousands of already-existing "stuff" paintings. It told me that sweet Jasper (that was his name — ironic, since he shares it with Jasper Johns, who had a particular knack for making "stuff" wholly unfamiliar if not quite abstract — he specifically chose to paint "things the mind already knows" in order to challenge what those minds thought they knew about flags, targets, maps, beer, etc.) would never be able to understand what I felt and read it back to me in a way that created a shared, but discursive account of things — an invention, a colored memory. When he fucked me into ravaged oblivion like no one had ever fucked me, even when they were given permission to inflict pain, it was also made nicer: "Just what he needed to get where he was goin'" — like a Rand McNalley Road Atlas and a fresh cup of 7-Eleven coffee with French vanilla creamer. He valued neither the shocking effortlessness of everyday ugliness, like spilled paint, nor the extravagant depths of awfulness, like alcoholic rage, both of which the AbEx painters were utterly deft at bringing to the surface like a rolling boil.

Admittedly, it was a bit of a test when I took Nathan to see the retrospective of one of my more pretentious and quiet, but most subtle and incisive art friends: Agnes Martin. Like Pollock, Martin enacts a knowledge of people, in the sense that who they are is revealed in front of her works. Works like *On a Clear Day* (1973) and *Friendship* (1963) were some of her most challenging pieces in the show. They're grids. On paper, "just" grids (indeed, *On a Clear Day* is actually a grid of grids: small grid drawings, framed and all mounted together in a larger grid formation on the wall), but they capture patience and restraint. *Friendship* is large, square; this and many of her canvases were made uniform at 6' x 6' — an immersive scale which has often led her work to be considered in the context of landscapes and spirituality. She reduced the scale of her works to 5' x 5' in her eighties so that she could carry them more easily.[11] She painted the canvases with dark brown-red oil paint the color of cinnabar, then covered them entirely in a layer of gold leaf (thin, but real gold). She dug into the gold by hand, effectively bringing lines up from underneath, leaving scalpel-thin trenches across the previously pristine metallic surfaces. Her grid works require close looking to observe the pressure waves: her body's signature inability to be machine. Her works record the minutia of quivering, trembling, shakiness, any minor vibrations. Working nerves. Her time and focus, despite her probable boredom and localized pain in her hand, make these gifts of sacrifice. She was so focused on her work that she'd sometimes eat only bananas all day in order to avoid the distraction of preparing, consuming, and cleaning up meals.[12] The completed works are usually grounding in their simplicity and order, or sometimes impressively, gently nauseating in their geometric repetition, which lends a paradoxical sense of motion. Though recent scholarship has suggested she was both asexual and aromantic,[13] her sexuality often comes up as something to be interpreted in the works, in part because they are sensual. On a canvas that strives for perfection, the imperfections become the most noticeable, sparkling elements. And they bring you close. You have to get right up to the line in the museum, the one we know not to cross lest alarms sound and draw bumptious derision from those who assume you don't know what those lines do. There, close, you can see her touch, the motion of a delicate, careful hand remembered in her graphite marks: a caress for lengths and lengths across the canvas, again and again and again.

Works like *Untitled #3* (1974) or *Happy Holiday* (1999) are perhaps a little more accessible. They are still minimal, barely-theres. The former is six rectangles, stacked 3' x 3', and the latter is composed of stripes, but they use colors that invite associations with sweetness and softness: hazy pink like the spinning threads of melted sugar becoming cotton candy; blue like frosting piped in a ring atop a child's birthday cake; dusty white like marshmallows that have gently exfoliated one another in an overstuffed bag. The shapes, however, are flat and sterile, and when taken with her other works, they waver between meditative and compulsive, interminable. They feel frivolous and ill at the same time, a combination I relish in processing, like a silver ball batted across the cabinet of a pinball machine by its flippers into the bumpers and bash toys and back again. She talked about her works being "a world without interruption or obstacle,"[14] which was maybe even more legible to me at that time from the vantage point of being in a new relationship. In that moment, they felt like us: cautious and skeletal; the beginning of something, but open and vast with possibility. He stood in front of them really filled with wonder. I was surprised how filled. He used words like "brilliant" and "genius," but without any art historical vocabulary or comparisons to other artists. He relied on his feelings in front of the works, describing warmth, isolation, and the comforts of routine and patterns. He got close to them without my instruction, and didn't trip the alarm. He related to me that day like I had secret knowledge for decoding and interpreting and he wanted it. He looked to me to translate, or to help cultivate the tools with which he could meld visual description and the physical experience of looking.

Our meeting with my other friends down the hall in the permanent collection did not go as well. Within a short distance of one another were a screenprint of two photos of Carolee Schneemann's ***Interior Scroll*** (1975), Rebecca Horn's wearable sculpture ***Einhorn*** (1970–72) — mounted to the wall alongside a photo of a performer wearing it — a photo of VALIE EXPORT's ***Action Pants (Genital Panic)*** (1969), and a table with a variety of props used by Marina Abramovic in her piece ***Rhythm 0*** (1974), photo documentation of which was presented on the wall next to the table. These are all works of performance art, and draw on sexual themes and aesthetics to varying degrees. I love them all, and they are all important to my work as an artist, art historian, and feminist. They are not beyond criticism, and there are works which are better (Yoko Ono's *Cut Piece* (1964) and Adrian Piper's *Mythic Being* (1973) are, I think, two such superior works of feminist performance art), but those were the ones we saw that day.

Interior Scroll and *Action Pants* both feature vaginas prominently. The image in the Tate's collection is from Schneemann's performance of *Interior Scroll* at *Women Here and Now*, an exhibition of paintings and performances held in East Hampton, New York, in 1975. On its wall label, the Tate includes beet juice, urine, and coffee under "medium". In the piece, Schneemann enters with significant pageantry, now a thing of legend. For me, recounting each step when I describe this work to students has become a ritual in its own right: in low light, she undresses and wraps herself in a sheet. She gets up on a long table in front of the audience and drops the sheet to expose herself in an artist's apron. She paints parts of her thigh, torso, and the edges of her face in what was either black paint or local mud, according to different accounts, strikes poses like a life model in a drawing class, and reads intermittently from her book *Cezanne, She Was A Great Painter* (1976). She then removes the apron, and squats slightly, with her left arm flung all the way behind her, perpendicular to her ribcage. She drops her right shoulder down and inward slightly so she's able to reach into her vagina, and pull out a scroll, which she unravels from its anchor point within her. In interviews about the work, she takes great care describing her design of the scroll's shape and dimensions so that it would fit comfortably, and the "secret recipe"[15] which she used for the paper so that, presumably, it would withstand the vagina's moderately acidic and dewy environs. In the Tate's image, the scroll extends up from her vagina to the level of her face. Schneemann's right hand rests on the inside of her left thigh as she guides the scroll upward and out of her insides with her fingers. The text was taken from Schneemann's film *Kitch's Last Meal,* which she had started two years earlier but did not complete until 1976. The text of the scroll lines the image in the Tate's collection.

The opening of her text goes:

> I MET A HAPPY MAN
> A STRUCTURALIST FILMMAKER
> — BUT DON'T CALL ME THAT
> IT'S SOMETHING ELSE I DO —
> HE SAID WE ARE FOND OF YOU
> YOU ARE CHARMING
> BUT DON'T ASK US TO LOOK
> AT YOUR FILMS
> WE CANNOT
> THERE ARE CERTAIN FILMS
> WE CANNOT LOOK AT:
> THE PERSONAL CLUTTER
> THE PERSISTENCE OF FEELING
> THE HAND-TOUCH SENSIBILITY
> THE DIARISTIC INDULGENCE
> THE PAINTERLY MESS
> THE DENSE GESTALT
> THE PRIMITIVE TECHNIQUES
> (I DON'T TAKE THE ADVICE
> OF MEN WHO ONLY TALK TO
> THEMSELVES)

Though the text describes a conversation with a male "structuralist filmmaker," it was later revealed that the target of her critique was the female American film critic and art historian Annette Michelson. Michelson claimed she could not look at Schneemann's films due to the qualities listed on the scroll: diaristic indulgence, painterly mess, etc.[16] Schneemann confronts the critique by exaggerating these elements in the work and announcing them in the text. Michelson probably also didn't like that Schneemann explored the vagina's physical and conceptual properties. In her own written texts, Schneemann described the vagina as "a sculptural form, an architectural referent, the source of sacred knowledge, ecstasy, birth passage, transformation."[17] Her performance provided a vehicle for conveying these ideas in a physical and shocking way.

In the museum's photo of *Action Pants*, VALIE EXPORT exposes her furry labia in all their glory. She's drawn the long zipper at the center of her black leather pants all the way down. She wears a black leather jacket with nothing underneath and sits with her legs spread wide. She holds a machine gun and confronts our gaze, staring directly into the camera. In one variation, she sits barefoot on a bench; in another, she wears a lovely open-toe black slingback with a kitten heel, her right foot flat on some vintage-looking Viennese parquet flooring, her left propped up on a chair to accentuate her flared center. The photo was taken as documentation for a performance where she walked between aisles of an art house cinema in Munich in 1968, wearing trousers with the crotch cut out to confront viewers with her sex at face level. The unexpected, shocking motion was meant to critique passive sexual representations of women in films, and now here it was, making my new boyfriend all squirmy nearly fifty years later.

The vaginas were a source of contention with Nathan. He said calmly and with some pretention, but not disgust, "I don't want to look at that." "You don't like vaginas?" I asked. He responded that he liked my vagina very much but didn't enjoy being confronted with a stranger's vagina on this quiet

Wednesday afternoon so much. "What about the power of shock?" I asked. He said he thought Martin's approach was more shocking, which I thought was pretty good, and pretty hot. I told him these artists perform self-possession at an extreme scale to bring into view all the small ways women are refused access to their bodies or alienated from how they're represented. "And who better than beautiful white women to do so?" he said with a smirk, in total sarcasm, seizing, unprimed and unrehearsed, upon the main art historical criticism of these works. I did earlier lament that Jasper neither inspired me nor challenged me. I remember thinking, "I asked for this."

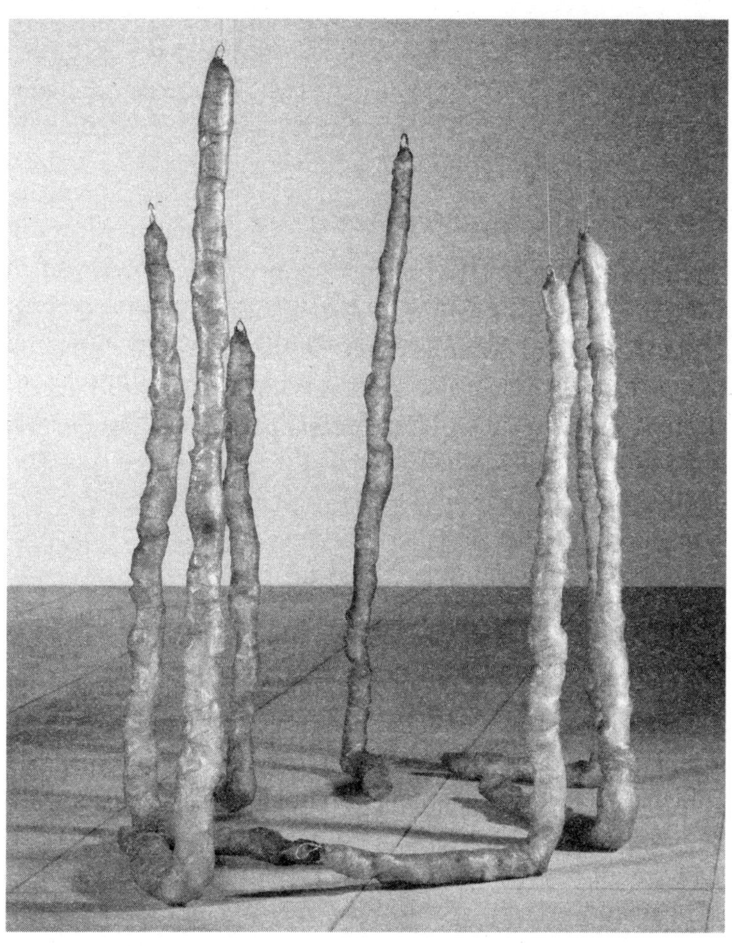

Figure 1

No title (Seven Poles)
Eva Hesse (1936–1970)
Fiberglass, polyester resin, polyethylene, aluminum wire

Paris, Centre Pompidou - Musée national d'art moderne — Centre de création industrielle

White Cubes

We moved in together quickly because he was kicked out of the same rehab center where the Cyclops lived. Turned out, drugs were how they knew each other. For years, they had run in the same circle of addicts and spent significant time together, both doing drugs and quitting drugs, doing meetings, trying to keep the disease in check. This was, in fact, the second time they had lived at this rehab center together. The first time had been about a decade before. Nathan had come back home to England, to a safe place he knew after relapsing while living in Bethlehem. His partner of seven years had re-located there for her work with Alliance Française. The relationship started to break down not long after, which prompted the relapse. Nathan's partner before me was stunning — a tall, thin, long-haired French brunette who gave off nothing but "totally has shit together" vibes, and who effortlessly married the fashion aesthetics of Cindy Crawford in the late 1980s to those of Jane Goodall in the 1970s: high pony, olive skin, collared shirts, matching neutrals, linen, shawls. Her apparent beauty and intelligence and the length of their relationship made me feel less crazy for loving this person, and like a good life together was viable; he'd had one before. Before moving to Bethlehem, they had both lived in Puducherry in India. They met there while Nathan was working for his father's friend, who was the director of a British-owned renewable energy company. The company had an initiative to improve refrigeration, specifically of vaccines, and it was part of Nathan's job to instruct people how to build makeshift incinerators to destroy expired drugs.

Nathan knew the Cyclops and I had dated, but when he said the Cyclops' name to me as if I already knew him, I feigned ignorance. Serendipitously, the Cyclops had left Facebook right after Nathan and I started dating. Facebook friendships were what fed into the "mutual friends" section on Tinder, so there was no trace that I had knowingly pursued someone he knew. The plan to make myself visible to the Cyclops again — to assert that I was not disposable, but was a desired thing he couldn't have anymore — had worked, if not exactly as I'd anticipated. The speed and intensity with which my relationship with Nathan advanced mostly obscured that goal, but not without calcifying the guilt that my insecurity and vindictiveness seemed to have catalyzed his relapse and expulsion. To be fair, I hadn't known these men were living together at a rehab center. I was hoping to date someone with an intensely loose connection to the Cyclops. I imagined situations where I might appear in the background of an Instagram post or get mentioned in some party conversation. I wanted to be a haunting apparition, an idea, not this; not privy to the tasks allotted to each of them on the chore wheel.

Nathan and I had been dating for three months and were telling each other, "I love you." I think that love was owed to a shared creativity, the requisite physical attraction, and for me, an excitement to be in a relationship in which I was acknowledged and initially very much celebrated after so many (about a decade's worth, save the aforementioned world's worst lover?) in which I was not. As his disease took over, his character became changeable, and he was often just very ill or asleep in bed. His survival became the sole project of my love, even though my methods were wrong from the start. The perfection of the beginning isn't really accessible to me anymore because all of it has been re-cast as an error, as false, or as a symptom of his addiction. I was the new drug, and then I was not, and the old ones returned. I thought about looking back at old diaries from this time to inform my descriptions, but I can't. If it was ever great, I don't really care to re-visit those details. I know I made art about him. One day I counted how many times we kissed. For every kiss I put a sugar cube in a perfect vintage white leather suitcase and displayed it with a little note:

Taste
Duration
Intensity
Number
Placement

1,2,3: A fast series across my face
4: Like at the end of a wedding
5: Wet. Feeling more of the top of the lip than the bottom
6666666666666: French kissing. You hold your breath in. Everything is warm and perfect.
7: A kiss on my head with eyes closed
8: On his left hand
9, 10: His cuticles

I'd guessed we might kiss a hundred times a day. When I began literally counting every time our lips touched the other's skin, I got to 325.

> I wanted to remember every kiss as sweet cubes of sugar pouring out into a room.

I already suspected that he had relapsed in the weeks leading up to his disgraced exit from rehab: I found a tiny bit of plastic with a knot at the end of it on my dresser. Even my very infrequent consumption of after-school specials and addiction-themed cinema — *Basketball Diaries*, *Requiem for a Dream*, *Spin*, *Gia* — had primed me to identify this as: *top of drug baggy*. I left it where I found it to see if he would remove it — to see if it was not meant to have been left there in the first place. He did; it wasn't. I described this evidence to some friends at the hotel where I worked, and they corroborated my assumptions. Given that he was always broke, we ruled out regular cocaine, and to our horror, ruled in crack.

This was my first lesson in things not feeling like they feel when you see them played out in the movies. There was no dramatic lead up. In the very beginning, I couldn't really tell when he was high, but in hindsight, the fact that he would come over to my apartment and nap and sweat until curfew (they had a curfew) was not a product of the summer lovers' haze I thought we were in, but tell-tale signs of routine comedown. The first discussion we had about his use of drugs, like the many subsequent ones, was initiated because he was caught. These conversations were mostly not explosive or dramatic until the very end, because each time there was so much disbelief. Only once or twice could I access visceral, lava-hot emotions. The betrayals which produced such sentiments took years to burn. I wanted to be the best girlfriend. I wanted to be completely impervious to panic, fundamentally incapable of freaking out. I wanted to fully acknowledge addiction as a disease, and I didn't want to set ultimatums. I rationalized that there wasn't a point in setting rules about what I would tolerate when I didn't know yet how those transgressions would make me feel. I thought I could handle it.

I will say the crack smell was weird. I handled it, but it was weird. I suppose that was a thing I identified pretty immediately as being off, even though fruitlessly seeking its source made me feel incapable of trusting my senses or myself. It was an electric or chemical smell, but not something familiar like lighting fluid burning off a barbecue grill or a flat iron left on by accident. The smell filled the upper air of the room with a heat. It's thick. Think burnt Teflon, a copier that's just done a thousand copies, or the taste — not the smell — of vanilla extract. It started showing up in the bathroom of the big house I shared with three exceptionally cool, creative, and clean Scandinavian artists. They were all androgynous and very blonde, with septum piercings and micro fringes, and they had parlayed their textile history and ceramic design degrees from Central St. Martin's into very high-paid positions as consultants, creative directors, and brand managers. I honestly don't know why they lived in shared housing.

By this point I had met a few of the other guys Nathan lived with after obliging invitations to AA, NA, and CAA meetings out of support. One of them, Conor, called me early one morning to let me know he'd caught Nathan smoking crack the night before when he walked into his unlocked room to borrow something, and that he was going to tell the rehab director. He wanted to warn me, he said. When he described the discovery, it was jealousy and betrayal that came through. "He knows crack is *MY* thing," he said. It was personal. I begged him not to tell, and cried at him; my emotion wasn't real, but it should have been. I hadn't processed the consequences of the situation, but I'd heard so much anger from Conor that responding with performed blubbering felt right. Conor didn't accept it. Expulsion from rehab is immediate. Nathan showed up that afternoon with thirty trash bags full of stuff. My flatmates sort of went with it for a couple days, then Annika — who was in charge of collecting rent and the only one on the lease — said something. I'd come down to the kitchen for a tea, and after I turned the kettle on, she said with gentle curiosity and slight concern, "Soooo…" as she chopped cucumbers for a salad. Her tone wavered a bit. It was hard to tell if she was going to ask a question or relay a group decision, so I interrupted. I said, "Nathan had to move. It was very unexpected, and I didn't ask because the answer couldn't have been no. We'll start looking for a place." We weren't close enough for me to explain anything to her in further detail, but she knew I was clean and predictable. I never left a roll of toilet paper sitting on top of the holder instead of changing the roll, and I always paid rent a day early. She seemed sympathetic to a situation that had clearly ruffled my little feathers. She just said, "Ok," and asked where we might look.

I hadn't actually planned on moving before that. It came out because I felt scared that she was going to tell me, or him, to leave. The fact that she accepted the moving plan without offering any alternative suggested to me that it was what she expected. The stress of moving set in quickly, and was compounded by putting on an exhibition that same week. It included photos by Nathan, photos by my friend Anna, the most recent videos I'd made, and my sugar box. The landlord let us use a vacant, street-level retail shop attached to the flat as a gallery. The mounting, curating, and promoting of anything at the gallery was shared among the flatmates, so this created even more tension and guilt. Given the impending loss of this space, maintaining some kind of gallery capacity wherever we ended up felt like an underlying goal of my house hunting — the space was something I felt bitterly entitled to regain, albeit at my own cost, and ultimately to my pretty significant detriment.

Nathan had described himself as a photographer on his dating profile, but when you read that, I suppose you hope they make money from it? That it's their job? His photography was alright, better than average. Sometimes he got really lucky — got the kind of shot that made you able to feel all your insides for a second. But it was not his job. He lived off benefits, and after a couple months together, off me. I had a job working in the events department of a hotel, and would also take well-paying gigs as an extra in films and TV series, which was dreadful. I'd never met so many people adamant about monologuing their elite expertise in standing around. It's also extremely strange to be so physically close to very famous people, and yet so far away from them in every other capacity. Meryl Streep, Colin Farrell, Hugh Grant, Danny DeVito, Tim Burton; if they were snakes they could have bitten me. For a time I got Nathan some work with the extras agency, but he got a warning for leaving a Ricky Gervais movie early, and then he was kicked off the books for taking pictures on the *Star Wars* set. Asshole.

In spite of all this chaos, the exhibition we put on together went well. People came, we got free beer on the verge of expiration from the hotel I worked at, and one of my flatmates' boyfriends — who was head of the MA photography program at the Royal Academy — was highly complementary of Nathan's work and encouraged him to apply. I was also able to do an article about the show for the magazine I wrote for, which gave Nathan some sense that he was a real and good photographer. He could have been. Based on our ability to manage his using and still get the show up, and because of how good the creative collaboration felt, I allocated a highly irresponsible amount of my university loan to get us set up in the kind of all-white, everything loft with hundred-foot ceilings and huge windows that would have made Andy Warhol himself cum Campbell's soup all over the walls. It was our white cube, which I silently compared to our sugar kisses. I thought having a space where we could make things and show things would be enough — a distraction from the drugs and something worth staying sober to maintain. I learned it just doesn't really work like that.

The Cyclops left rehab of his own volition. An actual artist for money, he had just gotten a high-profile gallery show in London, some commissions for a clothing brand in Japan, and another for fucking Levi's. He rightfully identified that it wasn't a very good look to be making art cash while living for free in a facility subsidized by a struggling Christian mission in East London. When he picked up heroin a couple weeks after his exit, he called Nathan — to alert him, to confess, in a way to share the experience. Nathan was still using crack, but he was shocked that the Cyclops had begun using heroin. Heroin is more serious, messier, dangerous; it displaces you in a way that, even more so than crack, makes it really fucking hard to resume your life after. We waited. We waited for him to say where he was, why he picked up, if he was ok. We waited to see if we'd keep hearing from him, or if he'd die.

Now we had a love triangle, or some sort of love trapezoid maybe. I loved Nathan; Nathan loved me; Cyclops and Nathan loved each other; Cyclops was maybe a little annoyed that Nathan loved me, because I think he had also loved me a little too; and lastly, Cyclops and Nathan loved heroin. I became the thing blocking Nathan from what his disease made him love, want, and need. I remember the night Cyclops first picked up: after his correspondence fell off for the night, Nathan told me he had no desire to use — that he had everything. I know now that, out of abject jealousy, he was just trying to convince himself, and me, that he didn't want what Cyclops had. I wore some red lace lingerie for him that night. Such a waste.

Halfbodies

I found that the disease cannot be bribed. You can't give it nice things to make it go away. We went to the Venice Biennale the weekend after we moved in together. I'm an art historian. I'd never been. Flights were like £50. I mention these details without really thinking, rationale seeming necessary for every decision as part of my ongoing apology to anyone. Since every decision I made for a year proved wrong, producing zero or negative results, the impulse to apologize is still threaded in between the details of most memories from this time. Nathan and I were to meet at the airport, as I'd be racing from work to catch the plane. He picked up drugs on the way there, either thinking it would make the weekend detox easier or not thinking at all. He missed the flight; I bought him a new ticket. He couldn't handle visiting the exhibitions the next day. It was too hot, he felt too awful. These short quips are stand-ins and summaries that spare you his elaborate excuses and our long-winded, futile discussions. He sat outside while I looked around, and probably would have disappeared if he'd thought there was any promise of drugs in the immediate vicinity.

This was one of the first times that a different kind of artbody resonated with me. I had forged my career, identity, and pleasure on the image of the commanding, electric, physically strong, and aesthetically provocative performer from a variety of media. But when I came across my idols, I increasingly felt like a disappointment to the very idea of them. I walked into the UK pavilion, and was met with rooms full of Sarah Lucas' slumped, failed, figures. She's known for stuffing nylons to create sculptures with gangly limbs which might be crossed or tangled in endless variations. The new works on view used the same stuffed shapes, but she cast them in bronze, then painted them in ultra-high-gloss paint, like a new car. Among the figures were black cats with dangling, over-used teats, which Lucas, in a video interview with a critic from the *Guardian*, went to the lengths to specify were meant to look "full of milk." The word "Engorged" then flashed across the screen. The sculptures looked like diseased ghosts, perhaps cast in their hard material as a way of trapping them or solidifying proof of their otherwise diaphanous, terrorizing existence. Other works included plaster casts of halfbodies: legs connected to a small amount of waist and tummy. They flopped over desks, chairs, and toilets in shapes that were languid and lazy at best, ill or dead at worst. "There I am," I thought.

As an artist, Lucas was quite literally defined by her youth. Michael Corris was the first to call her and her contemporaries, like Tracy Emin and Damien Hirst, "the *young* British artists" (YBAs), in a 1992 issue of *Artforum*. Perhaps because of their youth, the irreverent quality of their early work often comes off as bratty or punk, the kind of critical social commentary that lacks real knowledge or self-awareness. In their case, this is evident in the fact that the group's *sensational* reputation (even alluded to in their 1997 group show, *Sensation)* problematically eclipsed the more explicitly political, anti-racist work of the artists within the British Black Arts movement, who Stuart Hall described as "profoundly alienated from recognition or acceptance by British society at large" and "haunted by questions of identity and belonging"[18] as second generation diaspora. Unlike the YBAs, who rose to success quickly, artists like Eddie Chambers, Sonia Boyce, and Lubaina Himid have slowly garnered recognition — mostly in the last fifteen years, due to the country's extant racism and xenophobia.

The power *of* and problem *with* the YBAs was that they didn't seem to give a fuck, and they expressed that with their loud, garish works. This made for impeccable attacks on the status quo and institutions (they put their early shows on themselves in warehouses); even the hypocrisy of this — with significant financial and curatorial support from advertising mogul Charles Saatchi, who had made a fair amount of his money from producing campaign materials for the conservative party — was still sort of on brand: fuck it, take the money.

Their youth was in fact a powerful tool used to achieve the political effect of their art. Their willingness to risk or sacrifice this unrenewable resource made us believe in their total social apathy, and that more widely something must be wrong. In their work, they achieved this by showing their bodies and referring to ways of living that expressed a keen disinterest in their personal status or longevity. In *Self-Portrait with Fried Eggs* (1996), Lucas is slumped in an ugly chair, in an ugly room with two kinds of vinyl flooring — one checkered, one brown. In the back there's a stick, the edge of what might be a painting, and a mess of boxes or machinery. It looks dirty, but it also wouldn't necessarily look better clean, and probably smells of gasoline. She wears ripped jeans and a basic, murky green T-shirt, with two fried eggs over her breasts — a common visual trope in her work that mocks the feminine ideals which Lucas' flat chest, straight frame, and androgynously *un*-styled hair and make-up-free face do not comport with. Beside her are cigarettes and an ash-filled, crystal ashtray — the only nice-looking thing in the portrait, and it's halfway out of the frame. She is a rampant chain-smoker, still, at sixty-one.

Hirst is known for his work about drugs. His installations of actual pharmacies and numerous paintings of pills, or little dots meant to represent pills, resonate with the drug-fueled UK rave culture that peaked in the 1990s, when Hirst was in his mid-twenties and starting to gain fame. And, of course, Emin's works, like *My Bed* (1998), offer metaphors for her personal crises. She's a mess: depressed and probably an alcoholic, which is conveyed by the disheveled sheets, several empty liquor bottles, burnt cigarettes, used condoms, tissues, tampons, blister packs, and an Orangina, which Emin took from her actual home, exactly as it was, to present at Saatchi's gallery. Ironically, the exploits and creations of this seemingly apathetic, self-destructive group were lapped up by British tabloids in a way that was unprecedented for artists and which contributed to their celebrity.

As the old saying goes, and as every pre-flight announcement reminds us: you can't take care of others before you take care of yourself. These works suggested that the artists absolutely could not take care of themselves. Perhaps maybe no one could. Such a conclusion is an argument both for and against an art imbued with a more pro-active politics.

Lucas is apparently still uninterested in the longevity of her physical body. In an interview in 2023 she resolved, "I've smoked and drank all my life, so, if I'm lucky, maybe 20 years? I just think, well, I want to do what I want."[19] But in the same interview she described getting older as a process of becoming invisible,[20] and emphasized a desire to make the ageing female body more visible. I'm over two decades younger than Lucas, but her bodily sculptures, which sought to counteract the erasure of the aging body, also made visible the exhaustion and ache I was feeling. While hers was a remedy for aging, mine was for a feeling I had yet to name and needed to see to properly recognize.

When Nathan and I checked out of the Airbnb at the end of the weekend, he brought the key with him by accident. The host threatened to call the police (I think he was also pretty mad that we'd left a couple dirty coffee mugs in the sink), and I had to take a water taxi back to avoid missing another flight. No more weekends anywhere after that.

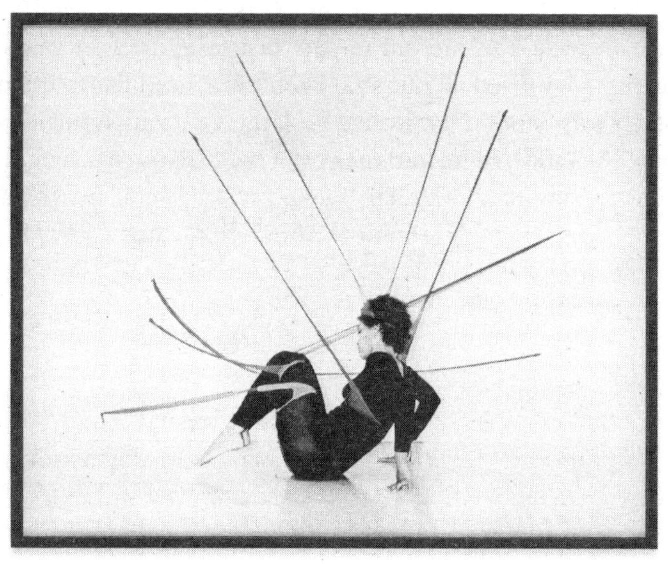

Figure 2

Performance Piece, 1977
Senga Nengudi
Silver Gelatin prints
80 x 101.6 cm / Photo: Harmon Outlaw

The Autumn

Nathan picked up heroin for the first time in eight years on the day we moved all our stuff from the shared flat to the new loft. It was September. I rented a large van, which turned out to be stick shift, so he had to drive. I hadn't driven a stick since I backed my mom's green Volvo station wagon into a ditch along a back road of Tenino, Washington, when I was fifteen, at which point lessons in manual transmission were made permanently over. If I'd known Nathan would be driving us and everything we owned around while high on heroin, I would have taken my chances with the hour of training my mom had managed before the ditch incident.

Nathan and I took turns bringing boxes down from my room and staying with the stuff so it didn't get stolen. When I came down with one of the last boxes, I found him vomiting in front of the van, bent halfway over, bracing himself with his hand on the hood. I was stunned and worried, and rushed over to see if he was okay. It is hard even now to entertain the memory of putting my hand on his shoulder or against his face. It makes me mad. It makes my arms flash with heat as I type, and my molars touch in the back of my mouth. He told me he was sick and nervous but ok. It was the first time I saw his eyes like that. I didn't know it was the heroin at the time, but there was just so much gray-blue. Almost a whole circle of gray-blue, with just one little pepper speck of a pupil. Later I would think of these eyes as the "eyecbergs." It was turning to dusk and the yellowy streetlight made all the little white flecks in his gray-blue circles yellowy too. He was wearing a black baseball cap I'd never seen him in. It was incompatible with his style, which, for all his anti-social behaviors, was entirely conventional, even prim. Good jeans. Good sweaters. Good shoes. A few expensive things rather than a bunch of stuff. No baseball caps. There were so many moments like this, in which I knew something was wrong but couldn't say what exactly it was, and certainly couldn't say why. My fundamental sense of things felt off, faulty. It was revealed over time that he adopted coverings like this when he was using. It makes me sad that he thought wearing sunglasses in the rain was less conspicuous than his tiny pupils.

The next day, he lay in the bed at what was meant to be our new safe haven and wonderland, mostly lifeless, apart from what started as a light, exploratory scratching, then became more: scraping. Then faster and faster. All over, audible scratching — like an emery board quickly filing a nail, times five. He scraped away some skin around his ankles and it started to bleed. I felt like I'd woken up to Jeff Goldblum in *The Fly* after he comes out of the telepod. There had been some palpable shift in his whole being, and I remember leaning over him, staring so intensely, mouth probably ajar, brow probably furrowed, as if the reason for this horror should be visible to the naked eye. Vomiting and intense scratching are two symptoms of heroin use. Again, I knew this from films, but I couldn't bring myself to believe that in such short course I had fallen in love with a man without a home or job, who had been removed from rehab for using crack, and who was now using heroin in a home we shared — and which I'd paid for but really couldn't afford.

Nathan convinced me he must have picked up *scabies* somehow — from the van, or the bags of old stuff, or on the tube — and he went to the doctor. Two weeks after we moved in, he admitted that he had used with the Cyclops right before we picked up the moving van. To be fair, he hadn't anticipated having to drive. I know at the time I probably still exuded the confidence of a person able to drive a manual transmission. He confessed after his flu-like symptoms became erratic (while remaining ever-present). He would seem normal and well after using, and then be sick again the next day. This was one of the few things that was consistent with after-school-special depictions of drug use: he needed to use just to feel normal, and his body very quickly required *more.* It could go from a £20-a-day habit to a £50-a-day habit in less than a week. If he didn't get more, he got sick.

As far as I know, Nathan mostly smoked the heroin. He didn't have track marks and I never found syringes around. It had a different smell than crack, but it put me in the similar position of constantly, consciously smelling my home. I get triggered when I pass by bougie, Goop-approved retail stores that sell a variety of matcha whisks and pretty, loose-fitting garments exclusively in colors named after rocks, because the sage they burn puts the right weight in the air and its smell is close to the smell of heroin: earthy, oily, warm, robust, but with a little sour twist to it. With sage, that twist is more like a resiny damp, whereas with heroin it's more like lingering notes of an oil you've just fried fish in. It's brown, and gives the walls of rooms in which it's smoked a little dusting high up. Around October, Nathan was attempting a controlled comedown, and was probably on two bags a day, down from four, trying to reduce by about half a bag daily. It was harder to cut back from two, because at the time bags were £25 apiece or two for £40, and like most people, he loved a deal. He'd also take some Subutex, which made coming down easier, but then it also took longer. He only ever explained the quantities when he was describing his comedown process with pride. I never saw him doing the drugs. It wasn't a secret, but it was *his,* exclusively, and I think keeping it out of sight meant he could lie about it if he wanted to, which really meant lying to himself about who he was.

He wasn't having any withdrawal symptoms, and he was topped up, so he was calm and acting like (what I understood to be) himself. Around this time, his friend Luke came over so Nathan could help him score. Luke made Nathan look fine. He was sort of scant and wiry to begin with, but he was extra nervy now on the verge of withdrawal. He had driven his little Mazda to London from some small town I forget the name of and which was three hours away, because he couldn't get his drugs there. Nathan went and helped Luke score, and then Luke got high (and clean, ironically) in our bathtub before dreamily coming upstairs to our bedroom and sort of flopping himself at the foot of our bed like a sleepy beagle. He had left a ring of filth around the tub and one of heroin dust around the upper shower tiles. As he soaked, wet and warm, he would have lit the underside of some aluminum until the powder on it turned to smoke and he could bring it into his body with another bit of aluminum rolled into a tube. He drove home an hour later, his hair still wet where it met his neck.

I never did heroin — never had any inclination to at all. The thought never even entered my mind until Nathan asked if I'd done some from the bag he had me hide while he was rationing down. Even then, it was like I'd been given the thought by *him*. I didn't mind handling it though. Hiding it from him worked. He never tore the place up looking for it, and I was incredibly proud of my hiding spots. The best was under the pop cap of a travel-sized hairspray in a ruby brocade hatbox of old costume accessories. I was equally proud and furious when I'd find his drugs in places where *he'd* tried to hide them. I found rolled-up tubes of tin foil in the pots-and-pans cupboard, off to the left where you wouldn't normally reach, and on top of the kitchen cupboards which were extra tall in our beautiful, dumb modernist loft with heroin dust all over the walls. I had to crawl up onto the counters and stand on my tip toes. Presumably, so did he. The tin foil is another trigger. There was a point where crumpled balls of it seemed to be everywhere, proliferating unstoppably like popcorn kernels spilling out over a lidded pot. He also shoved a bag of crack in a tiny little crevice where the brick walls were lightly weathered in the stairwell out to the garbage bins. To give you a sense of the denial that being in love with a drug addict requires, I just thought to myself after writing that, "Well, maybe that wasn't his." You do *never really* get to know.

Throughout the autumn he made monthly attempts to detox, and was in a pretty grotesque cycle. His body offered a veritable banquet of ways to tell him it didn't want the heroin he was putting inside it. He slept most of the time. His body was warm, but lying in bed face down, his clothes would be drenched in cold sweat. The vomiting became so frequent that I stopped asking if he was ok. It just became a sound I got used to. He lost so much weight, and there was often crying, apologizing, and depression. He did not want to have sex, and I did not want to have sex with him. He went to meetings when he could get out of bed, which was rare. I went to Al-Anon meetings weekly, and spent the hour I was there worrying about what he was doing. I knew sometimes he would meet up with the Cyclops, who I no longer wanted to know, because he had been the one to give Nathan his relapse heroin. But eventually even he wanted to get clean and took off for Thailand for the winter, where he thought he could focus on his recovery. He ended up getting even harder stuff there, and one of his teeth fell out.

Not having the Cyclops around to share the cost of the drugs led Nathan to steal. One morning he'd gone out without me; maybe he said he was going to a meeting. I went to the grocery store and found at the register that I didn't have my wallet. I apologized and left the pile of provisions at the counter. Back at home, I looked everywhere. When he got back, I announced the loss in bewilderment, swearing the wallet had been in my handbag. He must have been incredibly high, because while I was in the bathroom, he replaced the wallet on the kitchen counter. It was in these moments that the spell of disbelief and denial was strongest. I have a physical memory of walking up the stairs knowing he had taken my wallet, gotten cash, and bought drugs, but it just didn't *feel* possible. The thought of my love, my person, stealing from me was so unfathomable that it felt more plausible that my wallet had literally disappeared, or perhaps that I had never even owned one. I felt cloudy and light. I didn't even present an accusation. When I met him at the top of the stairs, I just said in a flat voice, "I don't think this was there before," and he opened, confessing to taking the wallet, using my card, knowing my ATM code. This experience taught him to ask for money when he needed it. It was one of the only ways in which he remained honest. Or maybe he just got a bit cleverer about how and when he stole.

In addition to my university loan, I was earning some money from my first job as a teaching assistant at the university, which involved some lecturing and grading essays at the end of term. I was so excited and *proud* to be teaching. I felt *smart.* I felt like I was finally starting my career at thirty, after spending the previous decade in higher education becoming skilled in doing only *this* while having no idea if I would like doing it. I was lucky and relieved to confirm after all that time that I loved it. I would spend a full week planning my lectures and editing the PowerPoint, cramming more and more details into it until the very last minute.

I managed to compartmentalize the fact that I was getting texts from Nathan during class saying he was going to die. Those messages took my breath away and intensified the fearful visions I started having around this time of coming home and finding him dead. Every time I came home, I called out, "Hello?" before the door was fully open, as if shielding myself from the potential horrors, diffusing them with the assurance of his usual "Hi, love!" The enthusiasm in his voice always caused such a jarring drop in the adrenaline coursing through me. On the day I received the darkest texts from him and did leave class early, he met me at the door in his long johns and slippers, with a green clay beauty mask on and a spaghetti Bolognese he'd made. "HI LOVE!" he cooed, like nothing had happened, clearly now high as fuck. "I hope you're hungry," he said, looking into a pot of sauce, giving it a final stir. I cried. I think my left eye cried with relief and the right one cried with horror.

My schedule felt chaotic because I was always rushing home — from work, from the grocery store two minutes away — to check on him, to try to will him into sobriety, puppy-guard the demonic essence from dragging his body out into East London to inhale more heroin into itself. The situation precluded social activity, apart from the occasional drop-ins by fellow addicts who were worse off than he was. He was generally too sick to do anything or have friends over. He certainly couldn't *entertain*, my god. Chat? Serve tea? Feign interest in someone's woes or endeavors? I couldn't invite anyone into our swollen home; we'd both be exposed.

One of the only things I did that autumn that felt social was have coffee with the promoter who had given me my first show in London. I had asked him for another show, and he wanted to hear about things — about how the new songs were sounding, what the live show would be like. I don't know if these were excuses because he was a little bit into me, or if he was just one of those very hands-on music types who, due to their position on the admin side, get off creatively on having artists talk to them about process and ideas. I'd been making music and playing in bands since I was fourteen. The line between sexual and creative interest in me had always kind of blurred, even if nothing was acted upon, sexually or creatively. I was used to the ambiguity, and entertained social propositions that I might not have otherwise were some professional opportunities not at stake.

I met Jon at a cafe only a couple minutes' walk from home. It was hard to talk to people. I was using all of my energy to suppress fears that I seemed to have all at once, every moment, ricocheting with actual force against the insides of my head: of Nathan falling asleep in the bathtub and drowning, passing out while smoking and burning the flat down, stealing irreplaceable things given to me by my mother, or having dealers over that the neighbors might clock, causing us to be evicted; or of him jumping out the fucking window, or overdosing and just lying there twitching as various fluids drained out and his lifeforce went the short distance from the dark gray he'd been existing in to black, nothing, clear; or maybe he'd just disappear forever — nothing stolen, no one harmed, no pain, just a sort of heavenly absence. Quiet. Nathan. Nathan. Death. Death. Nathan.

"FEBRUARY! YES! Yes, February." I was shaken out of my morbidity trance by the offer of a show a couple months away. I had successfully disassociated for probably a full six minutes. I'd had ideas tucked away since the previous spring, when I'd written the songs that I was able to recount to Jon, like someone pressing play on an old voice note. Everything felt sort of automated; I had to rely on muscle memory to break my fugue state and the chaotic internal monologuing. I sat there with my consciousness divided: 80 percent interminable panic, which gave names to the million ways Nathan might be dying while I drank Earl Gray, 10 percent barely holding it together and talking to Jon about a show and what had been, for my entire life, the most important thing in it; 10 percent taking account of his wellness and the wellness of everyone in the cafe, noticing that the horrible little place I was living in was so easy for others not to live in. I had forgotten. I didn't know how I was going to get out of this situation, but was reminded that the outside to my current inside was there.

I sent Jon several images to choose from, all taken while I was in Seattle the previous February, so that he could make a poster for the show. An old friend had taken the photos at the gallery where my previous exhibition was held, the afternoon before it opened. It was a massive, cavernous place — previously a Mexican restaurant with arched doorways and large windows around every part of the building that wasn't the kitchen. They'd gutted it and painted it all white, save the still dusty concrete floor. The image we chose for the poster was of me in a white bra and white skirt on a white leather knock-off of a Mies Van Der Rohe Barcelona chair. When Nathan saw it, he protested like a teenager, which is to say like an idiot. He was possessive. He said he didn't want other people looking at me in my bra. He was offended. "Why are you just sitting there in a bra for everyone to see? What does that have to do with your art?!" he yelled. I wanted to see if I could make an unsexy thing — a white bra — sexy. That was why. Clearly I had. I was always willing to fight a little, but not a lot. I never saw the point of engaging with him in debates I really cared about when he was using. I was later told by his sponsors that I shouldn't expect his thinking to be clear and rational until he'd been clean for at least three months — that the brain needed that time to re-set dopamine levels and heal its neurotransmitters. This was something I had somehow intuited by that point, based on his behavioral shifts and grievances which were progressively more entitled and weird.

Bad Blood

Obligatory protocol for a committed couple — meeting the parents — was fraught with further unnecessary chaos, destruction, and expense. It was, in fact, awful and dangerous. Randy and Bernadette divorced when Nathan was a kid, and he didn't particularly like either of them. Addiction and enabling were in his family; substance-use disorders are heritable, and enabling often comes with the territory. His father had been an early advocate and developer of solar panels but sold his part of the business at some point before it realized its value. He was fine financially, but he'd spent most of his money on a massive manor house with his third wife in the middle of the countryside in Devon, which needed constant and expensive repairs. He had entered his seventies, and had about a hundred grand in cash left and two children under the age of ten. He would start drinking alcoholic cider around 10am, and would go through two or more bottles of wine between the time he started cocktail hour at 5pm and when he fell asleep watching Beatles documentaries in the living room around 11pm. The visit to meet his father was only awful because I saw all the genes, patterns, and systems of abuse laid bare. The old man was so gruff and unloving. He was constantly yelling at his young children, like people yell at bad dogs. There was nothing they did that ever warranted that stupid, commanding tone. "Michael Patrick! Michael! Patrick!" he'd bellow from some part of the house where his five-year old son wasn't. What followed could be an order to pick something up, put a toilet seat down, or "come back here!" for God knows what reason. There was typically some mention of what "good little boys" did or didn't do, and what they got that he wouldn't get. "Good boys don't get their shoes dirty like you have, so you won't be having ice cream after dinner like a good boy would," and so forth. I saw Michael Patrick cry and run away and then get yelled at for it more times than I could count that weekend.

The visit to his dad's provided a look back at Nathan's childhood, which solidified the context for how awful his behavior was at his mum's. Both his parents were originally from Liverpool, and his mum had stayed close by, in a town called Wigan. Bernadette had done various administrative jobs, but I think she was mostly a wife and mum after a short spell studying Indian head massage. Despite Nathan's negative descriptions of her, I found her warm. She'd had a dreadful, emotionally inept, alcoholic husband, and probably lacked the emotional wherewithal to deal with it; I think she was just defeated by the multi-generational cycle of addiction I was then living alongside. She was preparing to move south, to Cornwall, to be closer to Nathan's brother, Eric.

She invited us up in order to meet me, to give us things she'd otherwise donate to charity, and to get Nathan to collect several awful collages given to him by Val Kilmer during a period when he seemed to have been acting as Kilmer's personal assistant, though the circumstances were never really clear. Nathan used the word "assistant," but it sounded like he was just hanging out a lot, and at a point in Kilmer's life when he could afford to shuffle Nathan types around via helicopter sometimes. I never wanted to hear the stories. They always felt like utterly ancient tales, likely initiated by using. Various figures from the Brit Pop scene sometimes came up, and when they did, Nathan expressed jealousy and bitterness that his band — which had never released anything and played only a handful of shows — hadn't received the same adoration as Blur and Oasis. This seemed to be the main source of his resentment toward his brother, who was also in the band and had quit unexpectedly.

Despite his mum's move, Eric would be dead in six months. He died from "combined drug intoxication" — a kind of overdose from the adverse interaction of multiple drugs — though there was some evidence to suggest it was a suicide. He'd done a degree in biology and told his psychiatrist in the months before his death that he knew which combinations of drugs would be lethal. He stayed at their mum's house sometimes, and she gave him cider in the afternoon as if that was an improvement on the club drugs he loved — the kind that don't have names but combinations of numbers and letters with dashes in them and which make you feel like beams of light are coming out of your eyeballs. Bernadette had moved to be closer to her youngest son, but why exactly? To help him? To keep an eye on him? To allow him cider in the morning so he wouldn't shut her out completely? Enabling is tricky. It was never clear to me how much to give.

Relishing his brother's failings emboldened Nathan. They hadn't spoken in over two years, and he wholly dismissed Eric as a "slob junkie," as someone "truly disgusting," "worthless," who "hadn't even been able to hold a job as a postman." Nathan said Eric had always been his dad's favorite because they were both into science and math. He got really intro drugs as part of the runoff from the British rave scene in the 1990s, and he'd also started making music then too. He'd garnered a small internet following, and there were more than a dozen comments on his SoundCloud tracks asking if (or suggesting that) the tracks were actually by Aphex Twin, and were being released under a pseudonym. It was trancey, techno, rave stuff; that's not my thing, but I knew the comparison indicated a significant reverence for Eric's sound and technical capacity as an artist. I never met Eric, and I didn't cry for him when he died, but he was verifiably smart and talented. There were no faults of Eric's that Nathan didn't share, but he colored them in the worst way. The disease made Nathan an arrogant, hypocritical fuck.

On the way back from his mother's, Nathan did some crack in a bathroom at a rest stop. It was a cold and blustery day, so much of the smell had blown away on the walk back through the long parking lot. I got just enough of a whiff to be sent into panic and doubt. I wasn't totally sure though, and knew visiting his mum filled him with anxiety. I worried confronting him might send him into a tailspin, and that I might not even be right this time (there was that denial again). When we got back on the road, he drove home way too fast. I got a closer look at his eyes when he looked over to ask when the car was due back: black covered over most of the usually vast, perfect circles of icy blue. While heroin exposed the iris, crack eclipsed it. He changed lanes for no particular reason at 90mph and shouted at drivers for their slowness and ineptitude. I pursed my lips, stopped breathing involuntarily, and held the side handle on the door, feeling anything I could say would be a dangerous distraction, and that he might even crash the thing on purpose if I told him to stop or that I wanted to get out. You hear the air at that speed.

The car wasn't due back until the following morning, but he kept up the pace through the residential areas of London like someone late for their daughter's wedding or, apparently, just really high on tropane alkaloids. I saw we were getting too close to cars on the left side and braced myself by scrunching my legs up and covering my face with my forearms, which I held parallel in front of me to cover my eyes. He clipped someone's wing mirror, and I screamed, finally, "Slow down! Please!" He didn't, saying we were almost home with a calm that made everything even more disturbing. He was driving in a lean with his chin sticking out over the wheel like he couldn't see the road well. When we got into the parking garage, I had a sense of relief, but I was still processing the drive and the fact that this man was definitely still using and had absolutely no sense of safety, love, responsibility, or care when he was high. Someone was in our spot, and he yelled, "Fuck's sake!" then sped around the tight corner of the rectangular garage. The wheels made a sound like in the movies. I told him to stop immediately and let me out. He pounded on the brakes and we both rocked forward before I exited, shaken. I stood by one of the massive concrete columns dotted around the parking lot. As he came around another corner looking for a spot, he turned too sharply, right against the column I was on the other side of, and scraped the car along its edge for several inches before he could process what was happening. I am still haunted by the sight, remembered in slow motion, of the column's edge grinding into that car's red metal, scraping it to the gray primer, and giving it a new flattened, mangled shape. I came around the column waving my hands yelling, "NO! NO! NO!" like I might be able to undo it, then covered my face and bent over like I'd been punched in the ribs. "Well, what do you want me to do, love?!" he screamed so loud that it was barely muffled from inside the car.

There wasn't a way out of this one. He could go forward or backward, and either way the car would just be even more fucked. He went backward, and I watched a scrape become a massive dent. I heard the crunch of car metal and saw the paint chip away before turning around, unable to look at what I knew would incur a tremendous fine he'd never even think about paying. Two weeks after we returned the broken car, they charged £2,897 to the credit card on file. I felt a similar sickening slice through my guts, and the air being sucked from my lungs, knowing just how ruinous this little mistake would be, but also how much worse, how total, it could have been. When we came up from the garage, I sat with my left elbow on the dining table and my face in my left hand for over an hour, weeping. He went to sleep. I imagined my face in the Cyclops' hands, and thought about how the attempt to recover that erotic tenderness was ruining my life. I heard the songs in my head that I'd written in the spring and hadn't performed, and recalled how far away my last show had been and how much of myself had melted away in the process of trying to wrestle Nathan away from death, trying to give him everything he could possibly need to get better. He wasn't getting better.

I left.

I went to Paris because it was close and cheap to get to, and because there would be art to look at and I could drown my sorrows in crepes. I ignored his calls and texts, and stayed in a cheap Airbnb that was painted an extra-light pastel pink and had sparkling white fairy lights around a little welcome sign hanging in the doorway to the bedroom. I did not fit with the surroundings. When I'd met with Jon the promoter a few months before, I was reminded there was an outside. Now I was in it and I felt incompatible, too long removed to comfortably reassimilate myself. How could I possibly exist in a pastel room?

After a day in bed texting friends and crying, I went out. It was still winter — cold out, gray. I went to the Modern Art Museum, Centre Pompidou and ascended its tubes of escalators like I was cruising through the veins of a body. *Untitled (Seven Poles)* waited for me, the final work Eva Hesse made before she died. I could exist in front of *Seven Poles.* It was as sick as I was.

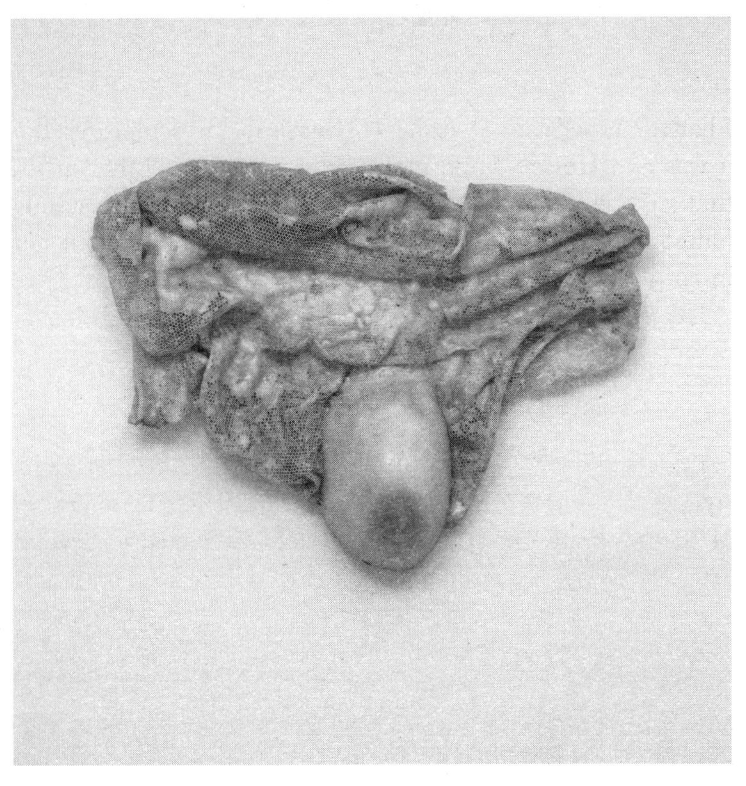

Figure 3

Tear, 1971

Alina Szapocznikow (1926–1973)

Painted polyester and fleece mounted on panel,

Ursula Hauser Collection, Switzerland, © ADAGP, Paris. Courtesy The Estate of Alina Szapocznikow / Galerie Loevenbruck, Paris / Hauser & Wirth. Photo: Thomas Barratt

Seven Poles

I had identified my exhaustion in Sarah Lucas' sculptures, but it was Eva Hesse's work, more than that of any other artist, that gave shape to the ominous, constantly awful, constantly haunted feeling I had, which forged new insights about her intentions and methods.

Hesse was among several artists who began introducing forms and materials into their sculptural work in the late 1960s, which explored some of the most provocative, messy, and unsettling of bodily qualities. The pliable, stretchy, or even literally flowing or deflated materials in these works marked a stylistic shift away from the hard-edged, managed geometries of the minimalist sculptural work which preceded it. Several artists and critics tried to galvanize the work with a bold new genre title. Artist Robert Morris called it "Anti-Form" and highlighted the work's embracing of chance and process and its resistance to gravity in a 1968 issue of *Artforum*. Art critic Lucy Lippard focused more on its surrealist, sexual, and humorous impulses, and called it "Eccentric Abstraction." She organized an exhibition of these works under the same name in 1971. What stuck in the early 1970s was the rather disappointingly less lyrical "Post-minimalism," coined by critic Robert Pincus-Witten. However, as the artists who emerged from that scene in New York in the late 1960s have been brought into dialogue with younger artists from around the world it's become an antiquated term for sculptural abstraction. In part, what necessitated new descriptive language for this work was the unexpected and experimental materials that were used to achieve their provocative forms and textures. Hesse was known for the seductive, slippery sheen of her resins, rubbers, and plastics, her never-ending experimentation with phallic and mammillary shapes, and her humor. She was also known for being ill.

Hesse was under consistent medical care for the entirety of her adult life: she began receiving therapy at the age of eighteen in 1954, first with psychologist Dr. Helene Papanek, then with psychiatrist Dr. Samuel Dunkell in 1959.[21] With some minor gaps, she saw Dunkell for thirteen years, until her death.[22] In the years covered in her diaries, 1955–1970, she received treatments for a range of minor and moderate illnesses including anemia, depression, and insomnia. She lists medications in her diary, including sulfur pills and penicillin shots,[23] both then used as antibiotics;[24] Demotil,[25] the brand name for Diphemanil Methylsulfate, which was commonly prescribed for acid reflux or over-active sweat glands;[26] Librium,[27] which contained the sedative chlordiazepoxide;[28] codeine, which she took for cold symptoms;[29] anti-depressants;[30] and sleeping pills.[31] The diaries make note of routine checks, such as dental appointments and pap smears. She also underwent several surgeries which required longer periods of recovery: a gynecological operation in 1960[32] and three surgeries between 1969 and 1970 on the brain tumor that ultimately ended her life.

Acknowledging Hesse's health struggles is key to seeing the production of her artwork as a method of care, rooted in the autobiographical approach explored by Foucault. In Hesse's diaries, her physical and mental health and how these impacted her work and productivity were a primary concern. She wrote frequently — weekly, if not daily, during periods of habitual engagement with the diary — about her moods and energy levels, her experiences of psychoanalysis, her medication, and her surgeries. She expressed an emphatic desire to be *well*, and remarked with excitement upon her infrequent moments of feeling healthy and strong, often because it meant she could work more, which made her feel good.[33] Both the diaries and her artwork explore the self and offer reflexive care. Hesse confirmed the positive effects of her process when she emphatically asserted:

> I have so much stored inside me recently, I *need* to paint. This would imply painting to be so [*sic*] emotional outlet for me which would be fine evidence to prove so very many clichés… I am overflowing also with an energy of kind needed in investigating ideas… This is a positive creative notion very likely I want also to encourage, develop…[34]

She acknowledges painting as a way for her both to release or remove emotions which had been stored in her — she implies — uncomfortably, and to channel an energy which she wished to encourage specifically in order to "investigate ideas," presumably to put to further use in her art. In this way, her work offered self-care through therapeutic release. It was also the kind of epistemological conduit that chimes with the model of care as knowledge production which Foucault explored.

Her habitual self-assessment in the diaries evidenced a need to be legible to herself, rather than merely an object of analysis for doctors only; to come to grips, in detail, with her experiences of embodiment and health. Though her diaries chronicle her reliance on a variety of medical treatments, there is a constant effort to define her experience of the medical in personal terms, and to navigate the power dynamics of how that care was administered. For example, one entry notes the difficulties she encountered when she sought treatment, as well as the persistence of her friends, which resulted in her getting diagnosed and treated. Written in sentence fragments, she explains, "Arrangements evidently not so easy… Dr all said depression, some sort of extreme depression. My side, friends, allies said No, test her, keep testing her, it is not her way, this is not psychiatric, she does not follow this kind of pattern."[35] Hesse clearly credits her friends with refusing the medical experts' reduction of her experience to something less than the urgent, life-threatening tumor that it was. She clearly expresses the anxiety about confronting doctors — authority figures with science on their side — armed only with her intuitive sense of her own body. Her diaries also demonstrate the reclamation of her body from doctors and institutions by producing self-diagnostics that range from vernacular, lay, or even petty in their frustration, to abstract and romantically lyrical. This, too, tracks with how Fournier describes forms of autobiography as institutional critique.

Hesse would have been just as concerned about defining her experiences on her terms through her work. Her sculpture, *Right After* (1970) shows this. Hesse was diagnosed with a brain tumor after a collapse in April of 1969. She received radiation and chemotherapy, and was operated on three times between the time of her diagnosis and her death in May of 1970.[36] Hesse worked on the aptly named *Right After* right after she was released from the hospital, following her first surgery. It would ultimately be completed over three sessions.[37]

The work comprises hundreds of feet of fiberglass chords, which Hesse and her assistant, Doug Johns, dipped in resin and hung from the ceiling. It appears to float, and was often disparaged by Hesse for being "too pretty."[38] Though its presence is spectral, its forms provoke comparison to entrails or old lace, and its sheen is inescapably spermy. Hesse's object is odd, but simple: it is a single structure, in a single material, of a single, muted color. She retains the use of industrial materials and simple forms — hallmarks of minimalism — but, whereas Donald Judd had the majority of his works produced by New York fabricators (specifically Bernstein Brothers Sheet Metal Specialties Inc.), Hesse used an intimate, collaborative, embodied practice, subverting the impersonal quality of the material, but also marking them as bodily and autobiographical insofar as she limited her forms to what she could make herself. This was an intentional strategy, confirmed as such in the writing of art historian Marcia Tucker, who discussed this approach in relation to Hesse's other plastic, fiberglass, rubberized cheesecloth, and gauze works. Tucker explained that Hesse modelled instead of casting or molding her work, often by "putting raw material on the floor, shaping [by hand], and adding layers until the proper substance is attained."[39]

The touching, shaping, dipping, curving actions which she enacted upon her materials became an extension of — or crucial addition *to* — the medical care she received, which in 1969 she summarized in language that could be easily imagined as a description of her work: "Bandage, wrappings, care, very tender care, time — vague, and very real things."[40] In her final interview for *Artforum*, with Cindy Nemser, Hesse perhaps sanctioned this mode of interpretation when she confirmed, "I can't be divorced [from my work] because I don't believe art can be based on the idea of composition or form… it is inevitable that it is my life, my feeling, my thoughts."[41]

The sculpture's suspension is also significant in light of the personal narratives embedded within it. While many have suggested that Hesse's use of unstable materials such as latex, which is prone to deterioration, acted as a projection of her own mortality, her friend, art critic and historian Lucy Lippard, describes someone who (after a second operation on her tumor followed by radiation treatments and chemotherapy) was "still optimistic, and as soon as she could she began work again."[42] Lippard explains that Hesse was at this point still finalizing *Right After*. Rather than a portent of death, in its suspended state, *Right After* suggests the hope of a body collapsing but held up, supported, and light.

Despite being made relatively soon after *Right After*, *Seven Poles* (Figure 1) relays much different, but no less haunting, sentiments. In it, the seven L-shaped forms which stand upright are bulbous and lumpy, but thin. They do not have the smooth, perfect geometry that I associate with "poles." They are anything but "too pretty." When I saw them in the Centre Pompidou in Paris, they towered above me, each pole six to eight feet tall, displayed on a white platform several inches off the ground. Like *Right After, Seven Poles* also feels momentarily suspended rather than static, but it works from below, rather than above — somewhere between phalanges reaching out of a grave too late and a trap waiting to curl around its catch with each gooey, muscular strand and lick it to death like a skin gobstopper. They are made of polyester resin, fiberglass, and polyethylene, layered around aluminum wires which spiral upward to maintain their shape. Over the years the material has darkened in areas, with casts of the very shades of mustard yellow, violet gray, and rusty brown of a large, but nearly healed bruise. From even a slight distance though, the poles have a ghostly white, cloudy look as light passes through them. The grotesquery of weathered, raw, aging skin is conflated here with the radiating sexuality of the materials' seemingly permanent wetness and stickiness and all the bodily fluids elicited through intimacy, illness, or violence, which they mimic.

Despite its sensual form, it confronts the ephemeral reality of the body through viscosity and deterioration; it resonates with death and sex at the same time. I call this the "Death Melt" — an aesthetic and affective property I've found to be shared among several of the artworks which had some therapeutic effect on me, shaking me from my previously too-unfamiliar-and-abstracted-to-know-which-way-was-up fugue state. In her analysis of affect — a term which, broadly speaking, refers to "feelings"[43] that sometimes elude easy description and range in scope (e.g., getting "the heebie-jeebies," having "a crush," or plain old global anxiety) — theorist Sara Ahmed explores objects' "stickiness." She thinks of affect as "what sticks, or what sustains or preserves the connection between ideas, values, and objects."[44] Death Melt might be considered a particular kind of affect, where the materially, literally "stickiest" objects are also the most affectively "sticky" — perhaps due to the reductive but intense associations which sticky substances draw to life and death, pleasure and pain. These are the things they stick together. And so what do you get when you conflate arousal and death? It's not a death drive, and it's not death. It seems to me a coming back from the dead, near death, or deadly. I think it's slow — a warming shift from hard to soft (but not soft to hard). Not a drowning, but a floating in failure and discomfort despite probable survival — a fate accepted like the post-coital lassitude which knowingly chimes with the French "*petite mort*" — the "little death" of orgasm. This runs counter to Ahmed's own thinking about sticky surfaces as something which are turned away from in disgust. She suggests that "stickiness becomes disgusting *only when the skin surface is at stake such that what is sticky threatens to stick to us*."[45] To be clear: *I wanted to be stuck to Seven Poles* — or rather embraced by or held by it, which I do not see as different from "stuck to," which suggests a secure togetherness. As an aesthetic, I "read" the Death Melt on surfaces of forms that suggest exactly that wet holding (that sticky stuck-to-ness): the making wet and warm of one body by another or by an imagined object, when presumably there is no one to hold that body, or when what needs to be held is so heavy and abstract that something must be invented to support it. Ahmed goes on to say that "to be affected by something is to evaluate that thing. Evaluations are expressed in how bodies turn toward things. To give value to things is to shape what is near us."[46] The affect of *Seven Poles* re-orientated me, and through my evaluation of it, re-shaped the events which had lead me to it. I stood there for about an hour, letting Eva's phantom limbs hold me without touching me.

I'd always loved Hesse's work, but I was seeing it differently. I was seeing the putrid rottenness of my fury, my emotional collapse, the suspicion and paranoia I'd lived with for months and months and which had rendered me nauseous and nervous all the time. It was laid out before me in this cage of gently sweating, petrified para-intestines. But seeing these feelings in some form made me feel better, as if they'd been taken out of me. In projecting my own presently dreadful autobiography, I considered hers. I bought a copy of her published diaries at the museum bookshop on my way out. Given my new relationship to her work as both a physical manifestation of all my worst feelings and, ironically, the cure for them — an acknowledgement and document of pains Nathan was too deep in his addiction to care about — I came to read her works in the same way: as what she felt and how she felt better. Her diaries offered convincing evidence of this. I began to re-read her work through an autobiographical lens, seeing it as both the result and method of her care. This book could not have been written had I not read Hesse's diaries cover to cover, experiencing how she produced a new kind of knowledge through self-care and the act of writing her own body. More broadly, her writing and sculpting of that body offered an utterly radical expression of the female and an importantly sordid, sticky new lexicon of what might constitute femininity.

Returns

Nathan's stream of texts slowed, then stopped, and I worried. I'd been gone for the weekend and didn't know what I would return to. I waited in front of the door to the flat for several minutes, hoping to hear some movement. Neighbors I didn't recognize got off the elevator. I gave the first couple a closed-mouth smile, head nod, and meek "Hi" when they caught me with my ear and fingertips against the door. I made demure eye contact at another woman, with my hands in my pockets, now trying to signal unthreatening, totally appropriate waiting. But most glances from strangers, anywhere, conjured feelings of culpability and the instinct to raise my hands in the air and hold my eyes closed tightly. It was instinctual to go home, but I felt maybe I shouldn't be there. I deduced that he was either somewhere I couldn't reach or he was dead inside. How long could I reasonably wait to hear from him if waiting days might also guarantee a version of his body, vacant, that I would never recover from seeing.

I entered and saw him across the flat, smoking out the window as he always did. He turned around, met my gaze, dropped his head, and turned back toward the window with a bit of a shuffle, having nothing to say or having lost the nerve to say it. I ordered a pizza after finding only butter and an apple in the fridge. I unpacked things and started the laundry. We went silently about our own things like we worked there. When the buzzer rang, he asked who it was, slightly startled. I said, "Pizza," with an uncharacteristic lack of enthusiasm.

We still had things to sort out. He scurried to lay the table like it was a real meal, seizing an opportunity to demonstrate that he still cared in lieu of initiating a conversation that might end in an ending.

He put his hand on mine after I'd been pacified by two slices of American Hot and some Peter Gabriel at low volume. He proposed that we go away over the Christmas break to Marrakech, so he could detox. We could sublet the flat and stay for several weeks cheaply. He knew Marrakech because his parents had bought two old houses next to each other there at some point in the late 1980s with their best friends, another couple — Rick and Jane, who also had two sons. They tore down the dividing walls and turned the properties into one big holiday home, with extended family and friends coming and going regularly. Nathan went out to Marrakech ahead of me to start detoxing (again) while I finished out the term. I arrived later to so much sun and color in my surroundings, and to him in a bed, withering, saying that his bones were burning. I kept waiting for it to be like *Trainspotting* — for him to tear up the room and run out and go missing for days. But no. He was just sick in bed, again. In that time, I wrote his application for the Photography MA in the department where our friend's boyfriend was the head. Nathan had become bones, poison blood, and bad skin only. I related to him as a shape and felt like I had to *do something* with him; at least try to write a future for him that would give me space. It was a down payment on the energy I hoped to get back if he got into the program and could be doing something every day.

We stayed the month-long duration of my winter break and sublet the flat as planned. The girl renting it let us know she was on a consulting gig and that, since the company was paying for it, we could charge a little extra. I think I took it up an extra £250 pounds a month. But her nonchalance towards others' belongings would greet me later in the form of a toilet bowl so defiantly neglected that it opened up a whole world of internet research on acid cleaners and mineral deposits. I also considered the possibility that she was an actual angel, sent to relieve me of some of the financial ruin Nathan was putting me in, and the extreme stress and guilt which came with it, along with the certainty that this was enabling and I wasn't doing what was right for either of us. I'm sure they don't teach angels how to clean toilets in angel school. This was further proof of my hypothesis, but also of my shift toward what Joan Didion referred to as "magical thinking." Irrational notions move in unquestioned while your brain processes trauma in some tidy and recessed compartment of the mind, because to bring that trauma forward would probably mean screaming uncontrollably for a matter of minutes and then still not knowing what to do. In Didion's book, she waits in her grief, expecting her husband to come back from the dead. I guess Nathan and I weren't married, so it was a little different.

We spent Christmas in the country with Nathan's friend Abdelfattah, his wife, Miriam, and their two children, Farah, five, and Hassan, nine. When his parents renovated the two houses, Nathan had done much of the construction work alongside a man named Fath Allah (who I'd meet later) and Abdelfattah, who now sold antique doors in the medina. I learned that the renovation project had also been a way for Nathan to detox and rehabilitate after another period spent using in his late twenties. The disease had found him in his late teens, and he had relapsed every few years since. Abdelfattah lived forty minutes away by car, on a small property along a dirt path which you had to walk down for another twenty minutes from the main road to get to. It was warm, and there were several olive groves dotted around the expansive space, which was undeveloped apart from the road, a small high school with fresh lines painted in the parking lot, and a little row of five industrial units with steel shutters, where a butcher and some other kiosks sold their wares. Along the dirt road to Abdellfatah's was an enclosed wooden structure, about 12' x 12'. Inside was a horse-drawn olive grinder: a blindfolded white horse walked in circles with a large wooden beam attached to its back, which connected to an iron pivot that would allow a large millstone to grind the olives. Oil trickled down a smaller than expected funnel at the edge of the stone trough.

Miriam made a tagine for Christmas lunch, and we had her cookies and tea after. We took a long walk through a neighbor's olive grove, and stayed overnight on the floor in the living room in sleeping bags. There was a door at the gate which led onto a large patio and directly into the house, which was completely open and without doors on one side. Thick curtains hung across that side to keep the cold out at night. To use the outhouse, you walked through a pen with sheep and cows. Nathan was still detoxing and a bit of a pill, but he was at his best in the country with his friend's family. He had some grace: He received food and care with gratitude. He didn't complain. He was just softer, with no self-pity or bitterness.

He had also found an AA group led by an older French man, Jean Claude, who became his sponsor and a sober, sophisticated father figure, who also had a sharp sense of humor. His wife, Mimi, was perfect — short and fit, with a haircut like Mia Farrow in *Rosemary's Baby*; she was a painter and part-time French translator. I told her that her work reminded me of Helen Frankenthaler's massive canvases with layers and pools of gem-toned stains. Mimi said Frankenthaler was her favorite artist. Both she and her husband were retired scientists. In the 1970s, they had spent a couple of years living in my home state, Washington, working at a now decommissioned nuclear production site. Their home in Marrakech was part of a former royal residence, which seemed like an impossible fantasy, but it definitely did look like a palace. It was massive in scale, but not ostentatious in its decor at all. It was all smooth gray stone. The columns in the courtyard were probably twenty feet high, and six feet around. The capitals that topped each column and separated them from the upper terrace they supported were simple, ovular, like squished stone lemons. At the bottom of each column were more robust spheres of stone. There were tall, healthy green palms dotted around, but the space was otherwise bare and unadorned.

After a week at a cheap riad we'd found on Airbnb, we moved in with an Italian man who rented us a room for €300 a month. Nathan had been walking back from AA when there was a sudden rainstorm. He started trying to hail taxis, but none stopped. Then this man, leaning out the back window of a cab, pulled up yelling, "Hey man, get in! Get in!" It was a simple kindness. His name was Giacomo. He was from a town near Bergamo, and the same age as Nathan. I think he said he liked Nathan's shoes and that's why he stopped. He grew up rich and had done spells in Bali and New York; he sometimes worked as a graphic designer, but mostly lived off the family money. His family owned a luxury clothing line for children. He could offer us the cheap rent because his expenses were covered by his father, who sent him there to prepare the house for sale, though there was no rush or timeline for when that should happen. A leak in the pool needed some fixing, some things needed to be shipped home, maybe the roof terrace could be spruced up a bit. This could be done in a leisurely fashion over a few months.

It had been revealed about five years earlier that Giacomo's father was gay. This riad had been his own private getaway where he would take lovers, and it personified every stereotype that a riad purchased and decorated in the late 1980s for the express purpose of hosting secret gay sex parties conjured up. As with most riads, it was open-air, and at its center was a small plunge pool with extra-long granite steps which descended into it from the back like a long ramp. A plush sofa, covered with the same white knitted wool and embellished with the same circular silver sequins as are used for Moroccan wedding blankets, lined the entire back wall. The bottom of the pool was covered in tiny metallic mosaic tiles. A silver square was surrounded by darker aquamarine, and when the sun hit it from above, as it did on most days, it glimmered in so many millions of little directions it was like you could reach your tongue out and taste the slivered light. It seemed like a little pool of some rejuvenating elixir. Surrounding the pool were oversized silver Moroccan lanterns and curvy white plastic daybeds that rested directly on the ground without feet, and which were each topped with a leopard-print pillow. The area surrounding the pool was exposed aggregate concrete, which gave it an industrial, modern look. In the rooms off the pool — a dining room, the kitchen, and one of the bedrooms — the concrete had been made ultra-smooth on both walls and floors. One floor was red, another a black-and-white zigzag pattern, like the Red Room in *Twin Peaks*. The zigzag room had a wall full of black velvet sofas. The poolside wall of each room was glass, with swinging doors and ornate arches in metalwork over the entryways. The kitchen was modeled after a Mondrian painting. The vast and tall area above the stove and sink was inlayed with an array of white and red squares separated by thin strips of black wood, giving it dimensionality.

Giacomo lived in the most ostentatious room. You couldn't have dreamt it. The walls were oxblood red. The chandelier was red plexiglass. The bedspread was black, the headboard was python, and on the floor was an actual zebra-skin rug. Our room had a tiger-skin rug, which we couldn't look at and folded up and kept in a trunk at the foot of the bed. Behind our bed, a geometric pattern of huge square reliefs had been set into the concrete. It looked like the inside of a mausoleum. Every room had its own gorgeous bathroom with a deep, black, stone tub, surrounded by antiqued paneled mirrors.

The dining room had a long oak table that would come to be surrounded nightly by a rotating cast of beautiful guests. Hugo was an architect from Spain who moved in with us after he broke up with Silvia, an interior designer who he'd been with for nine years and who Giacomo knew from university. Silvia then moved in with Arianna and Valeria, two other Italian women. The former owned the house but was back and forth to Italy, and I don't think she had a job, per se. The latter was a concierge at a fancy hotel. Their riad was close by, and Silvia had a key to our place. She would come by to check on Hugo, who had spiraled into a depression, and their fluffy black cat, Kulci, who was always escaping to a neighbor's terrace from the roof. There was also Angela, another Italian woman who worked as a designer with Silvia. Luca, also Italian, managed the hotel where Valeria worked. He was younger and so handsome and knew it. He came off as apathetic, unimpressed, and chain smoked. Since I had worked at a hotel for over six years, I wondered if he just needed to let go of the performance of charm and attentiveness that the role required at the end of the day. Then there was Giovanni, a gay architect, originally from Sardinia, who lived in Marrakech full-time and who wore a kind of broken-heartedness and pouted like Truman Capote but was never mean. Alex was an older, dashing French man who worked in textiles and had a house there. He'd come to Marrakech for the weekend about once a month. Sometimes Giacomo's wife, Mircea, would come visit, but she had no interest in moving out of Italy for any length of time. She did PR for a Japanese tea brand that was moving into European markets, and traveled constantly for work. She loved to talk about which airports had the best bathrooms. She had a lot of energy and was intensely chipper and chatty. She was definitely smart, but kind of a ding dong. Childlike. She liked little cakes, liked being part of this weird dynasty. She and Giacomo acted more like siblings than a couple. She annoyed Giacomo, and he wasn't terribly good at (or sometimes even concerned with) concealing this. I think he wanted the preparations for the house sale to take a while because he was quite satisfied living away from her. She leaned into annoying him; she liked it. Lastly, there was Rosanna. We had only been living with Giacomo for a week when we began to fold into this world. Rosanna was going to have a party, and did we want to go? "She's amazing. You'll love her," Giacomo said. That was more than I needed.

Nathan had dried out by now, and though he was still a bit sour and low energy, he too was intrigued by what we might find at this soiree. Everyone — which that night meant Hugo, Silvia, Valeria, Giovanni, and Luca — met at Giacomo's for wine. Nathan's problem was never alcohol, just the hard drugs, but he abstained. I drank minimally around him because

I hadn't shaken the need to be alert if something went wrong, but I also didn't want to be in another state of consciousness than he was — as happened too often. When we left, everyone carried a bottle taken from Giacomo's reserves out into the night and the narrow, winding derbs of the medina, which required that we walk single file. It was like a little parade, everyone having conversations with the person in front of them and behind them at once. There were quick stops to light each other's cigarettes, fix a zipper on a dress, discuss directions after going down a wrong corridor. The mélange of tiny little gestures, looks, and curious, impressed, complimentary chatter was symphonic and textural. It surrounded me, and dulled the sound and sense of the anxious, interminable lines of questioning about fate, doom, death, and money which were all that inflated my interior at that point. There was just so much physical and sonic vitality around me that it created psychic space into which I slipped and where I was held, not a contributor, but a parasite living restored on a fraction of the energy burning off these beautiful bodies every single second.

We walked in, still organized one by one, handing off bottles and greeting our host with cheek kisses, "Ciao Bellas," and complimenti. After an embrace, Rosanna liked to gently push you away from her, holding you by the shoulders and looking you up and down, telling you in the coldest tone of disappointment that you looked spectacular, like a vision, a Madonna. Her tone was so serious that it sounded like you'd done something wrong. Valeria turned around to introduce me and I was met by the lady of the house with open arms. She looked like Donatella Versace in Sophia Loren's clothes. In her seventies, with big bottle-blonde hair, no roots, she was so glamourous. Pin-thin, she wore a lilac satin blouse with matching jewels concentrated around her clavicle and decolletage. They descended into her leathery crevasse, where a black lace bra moved tan breasts up, up, and in, in, against gravity. She paired this with seasonally defiant, jet-black, polyester boot-cut trousers, held up by a belt with a large, hammered-gold oval belt buckle, which matched the horse-bit hardware on her four-inch, open-toe black leather Gucci mules. Her perfect, powder-pink pedicure popped out the end. She wiggled her toes when I looked down, not to inspect her, but in a gentle collapse inward, blushing, when her compliment of me (but directed to Giacomo) was: "Hai portatto la giovinezza..." You've brought me youth. I wanted her to be my grandma. I wanted her to fill me up with her electric aura and feed me pizzochero and Barolo and earnest romantic advice.

Everyone filtered into the dark courtyard. It had a tall stone fountain at its center, with several round, concentric levels into which water would bubble, overflow, and fall, gathering in the octagonal well covered in small, ornately laid emerald-green and electric-blue mosaic tiles at its base. The area was filled with greenery so lush and tall that you could brush the tops of the palms from the second-floor balcony that lined the interior of the riad. Tall lanterns around the grounds and strings of suspended cafe lights punctuated a night filled with cigarette smoke and the medina's usual benzene-laced smog with dewy sequin bursts.

In the adjoining courtyard people were already dancing to a gentle version of Nino Rota's "Caracalla's (La Bersagliera)." A woman in a white satin dress, with a huge bun centered perfectly atop her head, had draped herself over the shoulder of a man in a tuxedo. She wore earrings which spanned across her whole cheek and down her neck — a sun shape, inlaid with carats and carats of diamonds, radiating twisty beams that looked more like a spider's legs. The diamond on her pinky finger looked like an ice cube. A man in sunglasses pressed his face into the jaw line of his date. She was taller than him and wore a wide-brimmed black hat lined with ostrich feathers and a black 1950s cocktail dress with the kind of sleeves that look like they've just slipped off a bare shoulder and form a little curtain shape across the lower part of the deltoid muscle. She danced with her eyes closed.

Then the music changed. A man in a shirt with huge white satin sleeves with polka dots on them, under a black-striped raw-silk waistcoat, kicked the band into "Ready Teddy" by Little Richard. Rosanna initiated a clap-along to the beat, moving her hands in perfect time, first over her head then down across her body, and back again, twisting herself into figure eights. She took off around the courtyard and her guests followed, clapping and dancing in line, magnetized like compass arrows by her singular forcefield. Women kicked shoes off and danced in bare feet, swinging their long dresses around into flares of emerald silk and silver lamé. Members of the band descended into the dance line. All were separated, dancing their own moves, but moving in the same direction like a pilgrimage, twirling and flinging their necks back with their eyes closed and mouths open. Space was made and taken where there was none. One man hoisted a woman into a high lift from her waist as the chiffon of her dress fell around him like a widow's veil. She kicked her legs up into a sharp point, and stretched her arms down against her ribcage. The man holding her spun around twenty times. Nathan was never more than a few feet away from me at any point in the evening, but it was the first time in a year that the stinging thought of him was not at the forefront of my mind. He wasn't there at all.

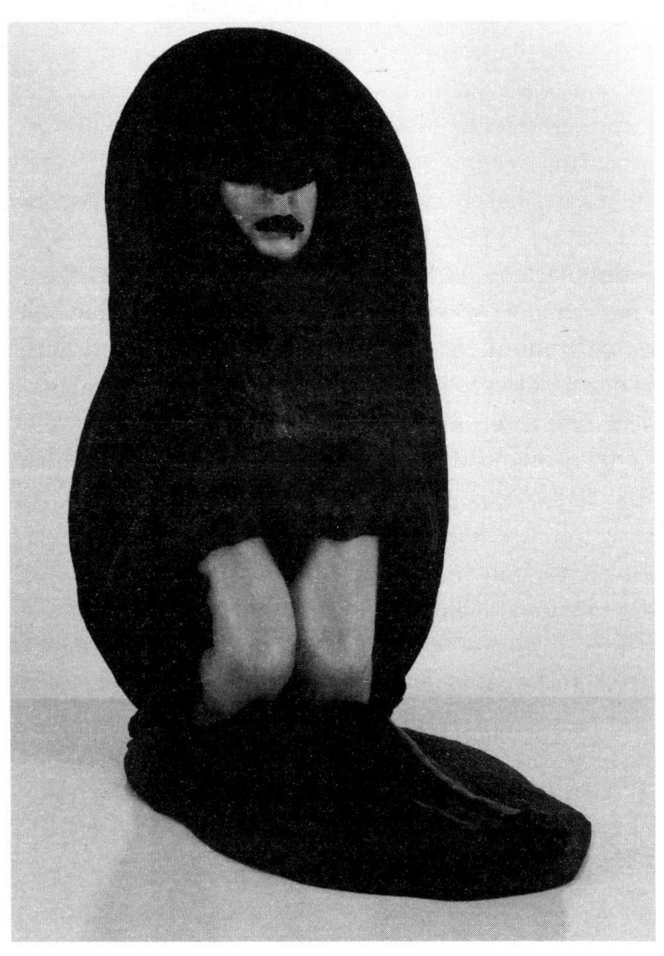

Figure 4

Stela (Stèle) 1968

Alina Szapocznikow (1926–1973)

Polyester resin and polyurethane foam

Ursula Hauser Collection, Switzerland and © ADAGP, Paris. Courtesy The Estate of Alina Szapocznikow / Galerie Loevenbruck, Paris / Hauser & Wirth. Photo: Thomas Müller

Clean

Coming back from Marrakech clean nine weeks later gave Nathan some sense of accomplishment, though what emerged was not gratitude or positivity, but a need to exert authority. He became a total shit. He was bitter that I had seen him at his sickest and most vulnerable for several months. He assumed a guarded, snobbish air, and often asked rhetorical questions that seemed designed to make me worry that what I was doing or thinking was somehow wrong. Soon after we got back, he also informed me he wanted to be baptized.

The surface of the church floor was so smooth and slick I imagined I was walking on a trail made of the tongues of all the souls buried beneath who were looking up, wide eyed, curious, and haunted (duh), with their slobbery open ghouls' mouths keeping the floor and the soles of my shoes clean. I stopped in front of a blue, inflated plastic pool, which appalled me in a way that the idea of ghouls licking my feet actually didn't. I didn't want this pool or this baptism to be real. The blue was crayon blue. The first blue you ever know. The water in it was still pretty, though. It looked like it was made by the sculptor Roni Horn.

Horn has made several variations in different colors and at different heights, but the signature sculptures I was reminded of were her cast-glass cylinders. The cylinders were topped with an oculus, which reflected light and objects like water does, though it was not water. I thought about other Horn works for a minute: ***Pooling You*** (1997), ***Ellipsis II*** (1998),

Untitled (1999), *Still Water (The River Thames, For Example)* (1999), *Pink Tons* (2008), *Water Double v. 1* (2013–15). In *Library of Water* (2007) she installed twenty-four tall, uniform, narrow, cylindrical glass vessels in a former library in Stykkishólmur, Iceland, two hours' drive from Reykjavik. Each vessel held water she had collected from twenty-four Icelandic glaciers. Most of the waters were clear, one or two were cloudy. It's still there. You can visit September to May, Tuesday to Saturday, from 1 to 4pm. I considered all these beautiful ways Roni had shown water, projected them before me, and tried to fit this moment in among them. Then I looked up baptism on Wikipedia. Maybe I could make it new to myself, make it new knowledge. Baptize baptism. This was more Didion-style magical thinking, but pretty next-level between this and the underfoot ghoul tongues — like when people don't leave their house in case their dead mother calls in the twenty minutes when they're supposed to be picking up their kid from school. I opened the baptism page and had to look up more words I felt privileged not to have been under the influence of in any capacity: sacrament, ordinance, affusion, rite. No. All no.

In AA there is a certain God factor. You have to choose a higher power to restore you to health and sanity, but you don't have to pick actual God, and you don't have to be affiliated with any religion. However, it's a common thing that addicts sometimes go full tilt on God or Jesus, and reallocate the time they once spent on their addiction to worship. Nathan was clean and that was great. I wanted that more than anything, and needed it in order to maintain any kind of functional life if we were going to be together. Although the work with his sponsor in Marrakech had not been religious at all — Jean Claude was an atheist scientist, and I'm pretty sure his higher power was his spark-plug artist-slash-scientist wife — the rehab center Nathan lived in when we met was. It belonged to a Christian mission, and they had encouraged Nathan to be baptized. He wanted to wash away all the sin and all the drugs. I think he felt that, now that he was clean, he could wash away every single thing that happened before and move forward without guilt or even memory of all the bad things that happened while he was using. The conceptual weight of the moment is ripe for hyperbolic visual description, but here's what I saw: Nathan got into the small child's pool and took a kneeling position, facing away from a man in a brown suit. The man drew Nathan back quickly by the shoulders until he was submerged in the water and then brought him out. When I caught him high a week later, he cried, not because he was caught, but because he said he thought it would work. He said he thought God would take care of him and want him to be healthy.

I had absolutely no idea what to do. Hadn't we just been through all this? In the next days, I went into a fugue state and went through motions. I didn't speak to Nathan or return messages from anyone other than my mom, whom I never informed about the severity of the situation, because there was nothing she could do. I stayed longer at the university prepping lectures than I would have in the autumn, when I thought the things I did for Nathan mattered. The only thing to do was end it, but I was still processing the shock of how quickly it had all dissolved. I had also let go of something else I loved, and I wasn't ready for another loss.

This was over a month since I'd met with the promoter of my show, Jon. The difficulty and failure of every day was compounded by knowing I needed to get a band together, practice, exercise, get the projections together, promote the show more, and ask favors. I'd had such big ideas: I wanted the girls I filmed the projections with to recreate and expand the scenes we'd shot for the live show. I wanted a little choir to sing with me on the opening, acapella, and then again on the closing song with even more instrumentation. These weren't manic fantasies; I had already organized the choral arrangement at a gallery show in Seattle during the trip I made home after meeting the Cyclops. But I couldn't. I couldn't dance or sing in the body I was in, which felt poisoned and hollow. I didn't want to be looked at. Being in stage light, singing, moving, had always been a way out of the mundane, the painful, and the real. But death had gotten its rotten hooks in me so deep that the thought of being on a stage could only mar that sacred space with these standing leftovers. I had allowed myself to be devalued and used, and had betrayed my ambitions and intelligence thoroughly. I did not want to smile through that now barely animate skin suit. I have played hundreds of shows in my life. That was the first one I ever cancelled, the day after I caught Nathan using again. That promoter never worked with me again, which I understood.

It had been nine days since his failed baptism. When I got home from work, I walked in and said his name. I could see an envelope on the table and knew I wouldn't get a response. I went to the note before looking around, hoping it would decide for me whether or not I needed to call Amy or the police before I went upstairs to our bedroom. "Gone to RAK. I love you," it said. I bent my knees gently, descending all the way down until the back of my thighs rested on my calves. My chin came in toward my chest and I brought my hands around the back of my head, lacing my fingers, like I was a little ball. This was good.

Friezing

The future of our union was uncertain, but we were both ok. He had returned to Marrakech, taken up our old room with Giacomo, and was doing meetings and more intense work with his sponsor, Jean Claude. We texted but didn't call. Messages were warm and encouraging but did not constitute conversation. Everything was on an unspoken pause. I had wrapped up my teaching for the year, was making progress on the writing for my PhD, and had been selected to present at a small exhibition of graduate work on campus. I'd thought of a performance piece around the love questionnaire that Cyclops and I hadn't finished, and which Nathan and I had. Based on this, I had limited evidence that it worked. I started going through it with friends, recording responses. I wanted to use the questionnaires as scripts for participants to explore whether it was the responses or the act itself which elicited feelings of intimacy. It felt fun. I hadn't felt fun for about nine months.

I also got a job working on the press team for the Frieze Art fair in New York. I could stay with friends, make a little money, and come back just in time for the exhibition. I got to New York on a Saturday; it was a day off before doing a site visit and some training on the company computer system on the Sunday. Just like arriving in Paris, there was this feeling of successful escape, if not total protection, from the possibility that something bad could happen while I was gone.

In the cab leaving JFK, "Sorry" by Beyoncé came on, which describes waving your middle finger in the air, telling some dude to fuck off, not accepting apologies; she tells the same dude that she's not thinking about him and, famously, instructs him to "stop interrupting my grinding." I know this because I took a video of the cab's interior as it played, a sonic snapshot or video postcard to my future self. I stayed with three different friends over the week — partly to avoid outstaying a welcome anywhere, and partly to see all the people I loved. All were artists working in different mediums; all knew I was in bad shape. Each cared for me in some way, tinged by their practices and mine. I went to Jane first. She had played various instruments in bands in her teens and had transitioned into A&R in her twenties. She had recently been promoted to general manager of a big indie label. She told me to try the Shiseido oil cleanser in the shower, gave me extra towels to bundle myself up in, and made me tea. As we talked, we started picking up instruments around her living room. I played around with a harmonium, then a guitar. She told me to hold still and took a picture. She said I looked so much happier as soon as I started playing music. After two nights with Jane, I stayed with Lap, who was an architect. He made me tea too. I got home from Frieze at about 7pm, and he fed me nice things and gave me sheets of paper from his sketch pad, and we stayed up drawing. He drew buildings and furniture. I drew shapes and filled then in with little squiggles and patterns. He liked to make popcorn for dessert. Lastly, at Gary's, we just looked through all his new art books. This was actually my favorite remedy. Gary and I went to high school together. He's the reason I studied art history at university. I don't think he knew it, but he was repeating some very essential care which he had given me when we were in high school, which was, incidentally, also a mode of knowledge exchange. When we were in high school, we went up to Seattle, about an hour away from the small town where we lived. He and I and our friend Sam were going to see a movie but had some time to kill, so we hung out in the basement of Sam's dad's house near the theatre. Sam's parents were divorced, and he mainly lived with his mom, who was the French teacher at our high school. Sam's an artist, and so was his dad. He had a huge collection of monographs in the basement. Gary handed me one on Jasper Johns and told me everything he loved about him. My mom had been a high school art teacher; I'd grown up with art and constant making, but I forgot that appreciating art could be a discipline. It honestly always felt too pleasurable, too easy to make a profession out of. But I did. It lingered as my plan B if being a musician didn't work out, but it informed the things I made. Now here Gary and I were again, looking at art books and sharing our ideas. He laid one massive book he was particularly proud of on the table in front of me. It was an exhibition catalogue with a three-inch spine that read *POST-WAR* in tall, red, all caps lettering. I grabbed the big book, which I ended up purchasing for myself when I got home. We flipped through and asked each other about artists we didn't know.

Working Frieze was being in the thick of the art world at its best and worst. Press needed to be checked in, and each outlet had to be taken around and shown highlights that their audience would like. I had to gently liaise between the press and the gallerists, who never wanted to take time away from talking to their clients. There were all these big art world personalities, all these beautiful works of art. Roberta Smith yelled at me about her entry time. What a treat. Jerry Saltz was in a bit of a flap because he wasn't sure whether he needed to check in at the press desk or VIP area. Posh and Becks were escorted in for a private view at 9am. Bianca Jagger always attended looking fabulous, and it was like a safari for spotting designer goods and archive pieces: vintage Dior saddle bag behind the coffee stand, pumps from the final Tom Ford collection for Gucci near the blue Rothko, a seated woman "wearing" Margiela's Les Topless Tabi (IYKYK) by a colorful little John Chamberlain sculpture. There were free brownies in the staff room.

Frieze moved so fast. It was energizing and distracting. It made it easy to ignore the fact that, in addition to my general emotional malaise, I hadn't felt very good physically since I got off the plane. At first I felt tired, bloated, and sort of crampy, but I figured I was jet-lagged and pre-menstrual. Then it started to hurt when I peed. Great. UTI? If Nathan has given me an STD I will fucking murder him? I grabbed some stuff at the pharmacy on way home from Frieze, and figured if that didn't help I could see a doctor when I got home in two days.

I felt crummy the whole week, but it didn't seem to be getting worse. On the morning of my flight, though, I woke up at Gary's and could barely move. This was different. This was worse. Extreme fatigue, extreme nausea, sweating. I took a cab to the airport, and when I checked in the desk agent could tell there was something wrong and upgraded me for free. When I got off the plane I went directly to the doctor. He gave me a urine test and told me I had a very bad urinary tract infection and should have seen someone sooner. "I'm going to give you antibiotics," he said, "but if this gets worse, you need to go to the emergency room." He added, "I'm serious." I'd had a few UTIs in my life, but a doctor had never spoken like this about it. Whatever he saw on my test strip or in my eyes must have told him it was going to get worse, because it did. I picked up the antibiotics, took them, and went to bed. Within two hours I was sweating and shaking, and I vomited my prescription. I called a cab and went to the emergency room, where they said the infection had spread to my kidneys and that I needed to get on a drip to prevent sepsis and stay overnight, if not longer. I was in horrible pain but it took me longer than it should have to agree to be admitted because all I could think of was the fact that I might have to pull out of the exhibition I'd agreed to at the university if they needed to keep me longer than a day.

I thought I was taking care of myself by going to New York, but being in the hospital shattered that illusion and confronted me with the possibility that I might not have known how to care for myself at that moment. My friends had taken care of me, but I had thrown myself into work four thousand miles away and embraced mental distraction so intensely that I was able to ignore an infection spreading throughout my body, and an infection that was, I was told, less than a day away from killing me by shutting down my organs one by one. When a nurse came around just before lunch time, he told me I'd need to stay another night. The loss of yet another show felt like a particularly severe lesson. I felt guilt, not self-pity.

Staying an extra night also meant I would need a phone charger. Nathan had been mildly concerned and somewhat sympathetic when I told him I was in the hospital, but he said he'd send the Cyclops with the charger, that he owed him a favor. For as much as I resented him, the Cyclops still had a piece of my heart, and I did actually want to see him. He showed up clearly a little rough, but who was I to judge. No one had, or has ever, seen me in a hospital bed. He had been the one using hard drugs for months, but it felt like I was the one who had failed, and who was fragile and sick. He asked if

I was ok, and I felt the edges of my mouth turn down and my lower lip begin to quiver before my eyes filled and I covered my face. I nodded. He laughed a little and took it upon himself to plug my phone in and pour me some juice. He'd brought me a Japanese fashion magazine too. We looked at each other knowing we had arrived here because of one another. We looked at each other still finding the other's face attractive, but with some countenance that also said, "There's something wrong with us." We did not try to make any of it nicer.

An Aside

In the process of thinking about why I wanted to write this book, what the goal was, and how I was going to approach it, I read several other texts which dealt with similar themes. "Co-dependency" was a word that kept coming up. I bristle and cringe at the word. While I'm sure plenty of people who have identified and sought to correct their co-dependent tendencies have been quiet about it, it seems to be a feature of co-dependency that it is easily made one's entire personality, something the co-dependent feel the need to announce early and often. I met a lot of them at meetings, but this also seemed a preferred topic among the extras I worked with. Due to the frequency with which co-dependency affects relationships with addicts, I do want to acknowledge it, consider it. I'm happy to accept that I might be in denial, but I don't think this relationship was about that. Some of the traits I have, most I don't:

Low self-esteem: No.

Lack of a sense of self: No.

Trouble identifying your own emotions: No.

Trouble making decisions: No.

Desire to care for others: Partners and friends yes, but

generally, not really.

Desire to feel important to someone: Yes.

Pattern of self-sacrifice: Not sure.

Non-confrontational: I mean I'm not an asshole about it, but I'll tell you if something bothers me. I aired my grievances about the smack-using pretty expressly.

An excessive sense of responsibility for the way others act: Absolutely not.

A tendency to fall in love with people you can "rescue": The literal idea that "I'm going to save this person" never crosses my mind when I start dating someone. Usually the thought is more like: This person seems to have lived with some dark stuff that will allow them to understand or accommodate my frequent moves in, out, and through depression, and the fact that most of the art stuff I make and things I write about are also tinged with a bit of gloom… BUT, I acknowledge that pretty much everyone I've ever loved would qualify for rescuing.

Difficulty dealing with change: No, I like it.

Poor communication skills: No.

A strong need for approval or recognition, and feelings hurt when you don't receive it: Recognition is nice, but my feelings aren't hurt by not receiving it.

> A strong need to control other people: I don't think so. A therapist I saw was troubled by the fact that I write my diaries in heavily coded language because I'm afraid of someone reading them. He built this into the hypothesis that I try to control people's emotions by hiding unpleasant things from them. I think there's some truth to this, and I am willing to enter it into evidence. "Let them be angry," he said.

I stayed because I really wanted to be in a relationship — wanted company, security, trust, collaboration, sex — all that stuff. He was smart, funny, and interesting, and after years of dating, nothing had gotten this far. I figured it would take the same amount of energy to get him clean as it would to find someone new. I threw all my resources at the relationship because I had no experience with addiction and thought that's what you did. From the movies, I also thought that if they got better, they stayed better. The possibility that it could get worse really hadn't crossed my mind.

America

I sublet the flat again and got back on a plane to America. My mom's birthday was coming up, and I had two friends in Seattle who were going to be out of town, each for a couple weeks in succession, so I could house sit for them. I knew I was supposed to slow down, make the tea myself, think about things. But being in New York had felt better than being in London, and I just wanted to be around my friends, and somewhere where Nathan hadn't been — somewhere without his memory slime all over it.

I let my mom mother me. She took me to Shari's for pancakes and gave me clothes from the discount clothing store Ross that I'd never wear but which I still appreciated her getting for me. I love the thought of her scanning the aisles of the outlet shop and coming across a red lace minidress, and thinking, "Oh, yes, now, this is for Ry." She was dating a man who lived on a houseboat and had a little dog. She was called Bella 2 because Bella (1) had been trampled by a family of deer earlier in the year. My mom witnessed it, and through tears, told me she'd never see deer the same way. I spared her the worst details about my relationship.

Her seventieth birthday was held at a bar called Character's Corner. It was owned by one of her best friends from high school, Vicki, whose mother had owned it before her. It looked like a log cabin inside and had posters from the Seventies around it, a pool table, and Skee-ball. At the party we sang karaoke and ate fried chicken. I was thawing but went into shock each time someone I'd known since I was a child asked me how I was. It took me a beat or two to bundle everything up and smoosh it down before an exuberant and committed "Great!! How are you?! It's been too long!" came out. My mom wore a red lace halter minidress and danced and twirled around with her beau. I sang "Jolene," and from the side of the stage a man joined in on a miniature trumpet with a little attachment that muffled the sound. Old veterans in denim vests with various patches and pins for service sang songs from the Forties and Fifties that were tinged with patriotism and homesickness. The thought of anything British couldn't exist in this space.

Figure 5

Negativo R1, 1964
Carol Rama (1918–2015)
Mixed media on canvas
Archive Ursula Hauser Collection, Switzerland and © Archivio Carol Rama, Torino. Photo: Unknown

R.S.V.P.

Back in Seattle, I returned to the Henry Art gallery, where I'd seen the Ann Hamilton show the previous year. Making this connection produced just a bit of Nathan memory slime, but it was quicky remedied by Senga Nengudi's *Improvisational Gestures* show. Though the body and collaboration are often discussed in relation to her work, care has yet to be adequately considered as a key part of her practice, and I was inspired by what I saw in the pieces on display.

Nengudi is a female sculptor from a dance background who, like Hesse, began working in unconventional materials in the late 1960s. Some of her earliest sculptures, which she called *Water Compositions* (1969–70), were made of heat-sealed plastic bags in elongated shapes, each bulging with water dyed an electric hue. They evoked the exchange of intimate touch and the supple squish of breast, belly, or buttock. This was heightened when they were first exhibited because she allowed the audience to touch them.[47] Nengudi has also emphasized the links forged between her life and work early on, saying about her production of these objects, "I guess that was the beginning of my sensual self… I really wanted to have something that people could feel and that had a sense of body."[48] Her description is important: she made these works at twenty-six, and here she defines a crucial transition into the sensual arena of adulthood as having been marked (or perhaps even accommodated or defined) by her practice.

A sense of intimate exchange with audiences and artistic collaborators has run throughout Nengudi's practice. Nengudi was part of the loosely affiliated group of Los Angeles–based Black artists known as Studio Z, which also included David Hammons and fellow sculptor and dancer Maren Hassinger. Nengudi has said of Studio Z, "We each had our own careers but our time together provided communal support when there was little support to be had outside ourselves."[49] In a separate statement, Nengudi further clarified the lack of support from white feminists, saying, "Hardly supported by our white contemporaries, including the women's movement, we set out on our own."[50] This confirms the necessity of community care and support in order to create artwork that neither museums nor feminist groups acknowledged. In addition to its members, Studio Z's community support also came from galleries such as Brockman Gallery and Gallery 32, and Just Above Midtown, which only showed the work of Black artists.

The Seattle exhibition featured pieces from her *R.S.V.P.* series — her most well-known work — which are further resonant with care and collaboration. These objects have been reimagined numerous times since she first showed them in 1977 at her first solo show at the Just Above Midtown Gallery in New York. Signature examples are made of dark nylons, which have been worn. This imbues the work with myriad associations: sensuality, femininity, the performance of professionalism, and fatigue after a long day at work. These associations could also be read as confronted or undone given how drastically different the nylons look after Nengudi has installed them. A work in the show, *Untitled (R.S.V.P.)* (2013) included several pairs of nylons in black, brown, and tan hues. Each pair was nailed to the wall, but some had been knotted together to create strength or strange embellishment. Where some pairs had been merged together at their waistbands, one "leg" of the nylons had been knotted repeatedly to create dangling twists at the crotch. The legs were stretched at angles into sharp "V" shapes, sometimes delicately crossing over each other. They looked like brushstrokes through space. They were held in position by weighting the feet of the nylons with sand — probably a few handfuls — which Nengudi has said gives the works the sensual feel of the body.[51] The sand was tied off into heavy globs, which were stacked on top of each other on the floor. These round weights, some punctuated by knots, looked like an absurd but erotic collection of breasts and testicles.

The series was conceived by Nengudi as a response to the physical and psychic changes she experienced during pregnancy: her body expanded, as did her consciousness. However, this was not the wholly jubilant experience conveyed by so many stereotypes of motherhood. Nengudi thought and wrote about the female body, and especially the Black female body, as a vessel subjugated in service to others.[52] She has said, "After giving birth to my own son, I thought of black wet-nurses suckling child after child — their own as well as those of others — until their breasts rested on their knees, their energies drained."[53] The tension and exhaustion she described are expressed in some variations in the series. In some, the nylons are pulled out to their very limit until it seems they might snap. In others, the nylons are installed in a bow shape like a caving roof beam, with sand weighting their middle, or are pinned to the wall, sagging like breasts.

The title, *R.S.V.P.*, asks the viewer to respond to the works — one of its collaborative aspects. Similar to how she invited viewers to touch her water sculptures to have a sensual experience of the bodily, Nengudi has described the engagement with the *R.S.V.P.* series as a procreative encounter, saying, "I find it very sensual, very creative, this interaction… when someone views my work I think about the fact that there's this threesome that happens: I interact with you and then this third thing happens — in human relationships that could result in a child."[54] Her collaborations with Maren Hassinger demonstrate how the sculpture is meant to work. Hassinger's responses to *R.S.V.P.* (she has performed with the works numerous times) involve her moving in, among, through the nylons, touching them, lifting them, wrapping her body around them in delicate, tangled, yet always intentional and controlled ways (Figure 2). Hassinger's collaborations move the work into the genres of performance, dance, and ritual. This both births that "third thing" Nengudi referred to, and offered Nengudi and Hassinger a re-birth of their identities as dancers. Both gave up their formal dance training due to a lack of institutional recognition and support, but the *R.S.V.P.* collaborations offered a chance to recover and reconnect with a practice at the foundation of their creative lives. In addition to Hassinger's engagement with the sculptures, Nengudi has also performed introductory "rites" before Hassinger begins a performance. These have included sharply contoured movements close to the ground and exaggerated facial expressions which recall traditions of Butoh — a Japanese dance form typified by slow movements and grotesque imagery, which she has often cited as inspirational.[55]

Other writers have considered the support offered by the pair's decades-long collaboration, but it's often framed as support for each other's practices.[56] Weber notes the general "intimacy and meaning of their shared path."[57] I suppose as part of my own response to *R.S.V.P.*, I want to look more explicitly at how Hassinger's engagement with *R.S.V.P.* also explores and represents post-natal care, necessitated by the feelings of exhaustion and extreme personal change related to motherhood and complicated by a feminist politics entangled in the workings of healthcare.

This work followed a period of renewed attention to natural childbirth in the 1950s and '60s in America, due to rising criticism of hospital care and structures. Reports of cruelty in maternity units could be found in popular periodicals,[58] while studies also found that upper- and middle-class women were treated better by physicians and hospital staff.[59] The Women's Health Movement also coalesced in the 1960s, which responded to related concerns. They identified their reproductive capacity as the main source of their oppression because the means to control their reproductive potential was determined not only by the government, but by the preponderance of males in the top ranks of the healthcare industry.[60] The publication of *Our Bodies, Ourselves* by the Boston Women's Health Book Collective sought to offer women information about their bodies which was produced and circulated outside these patriarchal frameworks. However, these attacks on the status of reproductive health became part of the same women's movement of the 1970s that Nengudi felt herself to be excluded from. So while her work's exploration of pregnancy from outside an institutional setting — a gallery — confronts or corrects the negative maternal experiences being located within those institutional arenas, it is perhaps especially when we see the work in the hands, and among the limbs of her friend and fellow Black artist Hassinger that the post-natal care of the Black female body is necessarily distanced from a feminist movement that was also skeptical of medical institutions, but a movement that Nengudi did not feel herself supported by. Indeed, in Nengudi's archives (held by the Smithsonian Museum) there is a photo of her son and an order form from the hospital photo service[61] suggesting that Nengudi delivered him in a hospital despite the increased feminist interest in natural births at the time.

The significance of a work which represents the Black maternal body and tender post-natal care is also brought into sharp relief by the histories of forced sterilization of Black women in the United States. Racist eugenic theories were revived in the 1960s, and Black women fell victim to widespread sterilization abuse at the hands of government-paid doctors.[62] During the 1970s, sterilization became the most rapidly growing form of birth control in the United States, rising from 200,000 cases in 1970 to 700,000 in 1980.[63] It was a common belief among Black people in the South that Black women were routinely sterilized without their informed consent and for no valid medical reason.[64]

There is also evidence to suggest that Nengudi would have believed Hassinger's actions to have had tangible effects — on her (Nengudi's) body, and as a kind of broader social healing ritual. Her interest in care, and specifically healing, which falls outside conventional medical practices, is at the core of her identity. Nengudi changed her name in 1974, the same year her first son was born. In an interview with curator Elissa Auther, Nengudi explained that her adopted surname means "a woman who comes to power as a healer."[65] She has also called other collaborative performances "rituals" and "healing processes,"[66] though the effects are described as somewhat less specific, direct and personal. Author and curator, Stephanie Weber has explained that "her definition of 'ritual' is broad, more or less equivalent to 'culture' or 'ideology' and their 'all encompassing' scope."[67] Nengudi's own definition supports this summary. She has called ritual "doing something together to make something else happen to improve your circumstance… [they] build up positive energy so that everyone can be better for it."[68] By contrast, her sand works have been heavily inspired by Native American sand paintings, described by her as having more personal healing properties that might more commonly be associated with care. She has explained that "a person that is ill, physically or mentally, is put in the middle of this sand painting, and it acts as a cleanser. It cleanses them of whatever malady they have."[69] Nengudi experimented daily with the production of miniature versions, and found the rituals effective, saying she was calmed by the process.[70] Although sand is not "sticky," it has also been described by scholars of Nengudi's work in ways that bring its affective properties into close dialogue with Hesse and Ahmed's attention to material and conceptual "stickiness." Art historian, Kellie Jones has noted that "sand clings to bodies and objects, can be intrusive and irritating, yet it can also be referential, holding environmental memories."[71] She draws connections between Nengudi's use of sand and diasporic communities, inclusive of members of Studio Z, for whom sand's immediate relationship to beach and ocean recall histories of "transatlantic specificity" and "the oceanic,"[72] presumably inclusive of histories of forced migrations, but also fluidity and immense force. The way Nengudi's practice brings materials and layered, complex personal and historical narratives together exemplifies the "stickiness" of affect described by Ahmed. Nengudi has gone on to create several large-scale sand works, including the recent *Sandmining* (2020), installed in 2023 at Dia: Beacon — evidencing that healing, ritual, and care are still active concerns and methods in her practice.

The risk of identifying care as a crucial aim and effect of the artists' practices that I have looked at was that this would be read as a sexist reduction of the work. Care has historically been associated with the "feminine" and with caretaking; it has been tied in with the domestic sphere and women's centrality in reproduction.[73] Because of this, it has been marginalized as "women's work" and undervalued because of the wider devaluation of women. Although I do wish to correct any notion that care stems naturally from women or the feminine, I also wish to recover the value of care as a ungendered practice and *art* that is at its most effective when it recognizes our interdependencies. Political theorist Joan Tronto distinguishes between "caring for," which includes the physical aspects of hands-on care, "caring about," which describes our emotional investment in and attachment to others, and "caring with," which describes how we mobilize politically in order to transform our world.[74] Through her work's incorporation of physical and psychic exchange, her collaborative approach, and the wider social impact she strives for with her "rituals," Nengudi's work offers a model of care that captures the methods identified by Tronto and recognizes the interdependent nature of care.

California

Three weeks into my trip, Nathan informed me that he would like to visit. I suggested that we meet in Los Angeles for a little bit and see how things go, then I would go back to Seattle and he back to Marrakech, or London if he was ready. I knew he had friends in recovery in LA who could support him and go to meetings with him, and I'd already planned to visit before I returned to London, because with less than a year on my student visa left, I wanted to consider it as a place I might move to after graduation. I put a post out on socials asking friends if they had leads on short-term rentals. Jake, a friend of a friend, offered me his apartment for three weeks for pretty cheap. He was a freelance writer, but things had been a little slow, so he was going to stay with his girlfriend for the month. When Nathan arrived, it felt like a scene from an old Hollywood movie where a husband comes home from war. He had been in sunny Marrakech for the last couple months and had color back in his face and meat back on his bones. He smiled, holding a suitcase in one hand that tilted his frame. He had on cool tortoise shell Ray-Bans, and the light hit him like a fucking movie star.

I wore pretty dresses. We did things. One of his friends was a DJ at a dive bar where we drank cokes and danced. We went to all the museums. He went to meetings and everyone met up at the diner in Los Feliz after for fries and shakes. They all spoke so positively and hopefully, even about little things — another week sober, a side hustle selling used books, a recipe for alcohol-free tiramisu. I exercised and worked on my thesis in air-conditioned coffee shops. We had really good sex.

On my way back from a morning Pilates class, I saw Nathan just outside the apartment building walking towards me. His shoulders were raised slightly like he'd just batted a spider off his neck, and his arms came away from his ribcage at an angle that was barely perceptible, but which signaled a tensing up of his muscles, a fright. I started, "Hey, what's u—".

"He's *dead*," he interrupted, his voice cracking as it raised in volume, making the horrible declaration. It seemed to me like he had found an actual dead person in the apartment. The terrified questions sped out of my mouth, "Who? Who's dead, love? What's going on?!" "Eric. My little brother, my baby brother. He's dead," Nathan said, like it was all one word. I flung my arms around him, fast and too hard. I was trying to physically stop him from picking up rather than console him. He told me he needed a cigarette, then changed his mind. He had quit smoking along with everything else. We went back inside, and he told me he had gotten a video call from his mum, and when he answered both his parents were on the screen to tell him. Eric hadn't been answering his phone, so his mum went over to his flat after a day, had the building manager open it, and found him. Neither of his parents were cogent. His father couldn't speak through his tears, but was trying to hold his breath to stifle the sound of crying, and his mother was spinning. "Nathan, he was just so..." his mother lost her words, on the verge of hyperventilation as she spoke it and made it real, "So cold."

We were still repairing our relationship, and I didn't want to go back to England but didn't feel like I had a choice. His parents didn't know anything certain yet about cause or arrangements, but we needed to get back to the UK as soon as possible. It was Monday. I moved both of our return tickets to Thursday through the airline's bereavement policy (airlines have bereavement policies). I called Jake, and he was incredibly understanding. He said he'd come by whenever was convenient to drop off a refund since we'd be leaving early.

Nathan and I held still through the afternoon and evening. In the morning, he left for a meeting at his usual spot, the Hollywood Lutheran. I worried he was going to pick up, but resolved that I didn't have any control over it. When he came back, he talked me through the meeting and how he was feeling; he was wearing his grief, but he wasn't high. He'd had periodic pain from a rogue wisdom tooth pushing through late, but unsurprisingly, I hadn't heard about it in several months, as the heroin pretty much took care of the pain. He said it was bad, so I went out for an oral anesthetic for him. I took this complaint about feeling as a good sign. I brought back some dumb, expensive California salads for lunch. Grief could only feed on bland food. We watched Netflix in bed, and he took calls from various family members with updates. It turned to evening and he took a long shower. When he got out he wanted to make love. He turned out the lights but asked if we could watch pornography, which he never had before. Everything we did was slower, measured, relished in. New parts of the body became important: knees, knuckles, and the cubital fossa (the name for the inside of the elbow, which I couldn't resist including). The couple on the computer screen were pounding at each other like butchers tenderizing skirt steak, but he seemed less interested in them as a model of speed and filth than as a permissive symbol which let sex fill the space in a way that I hadn't found customary for British men in general.

In the morning, he left again for a meeting. I texted him that I could meet him after, and we could grab coffee and walk home together. He said ok. I texted back to ask what time the meeting ended, and he didn't respond. Some meetings are an hour, some an hour and a half, and I wasn't sure what time it had started. I looked up the schedule online and saw that it was a women's only meeting. A women's. Only. Meeting. To his credit, he met me out front at the correct time the meeting ended. I asked how it was, giving him the opportunity to say anything other than what he did, which was, "Great." I stopped walking and looked up at him in the church parking lot, already feeling the muscles in my neck tense up to hold back tears. I was so fucking sick of that feeling, and so fucking sick of crying for this man. "Nathan, I had to look up the schedule when you didn't get back to me about time. It was a women's meeting," I said in quiet indictment. As subtly as I could, I looked around, using my gaze to direct his attention to the few women beginning to filter toward their cars, and the others collected around the entrance to the church, talking and smoking in a little circle. "What was it?" I asked. "Just some crack, just a little bit, just for right now," he said, with his face down, shifting uncomfortably. I was deeply relieved that it was crack and not heroin; this was how low my bar was. I told him he needed to go to a meeting, which he wanted also. We went to three together that day, making the rounds between AA and NA and CA — whatever we could walk to, whatever was happening next. We went home and didn't eat dinner.

Nathan left the apartment in the morning before the sun was up. I was basically still asleep and have only a vague recollection of his departure, which is still more a dream to me than something real that happened. I was not in any state to stop him, or even conscious enough to know that he needed to be stopped. When he got back, he said he'd gone out for cigarettes. I couldn't engage. He was in extreme grief and going into intermittent fits of weeping, and was taking call after call with distraught family members for the third day in a row.

When Jake came by with the rent refund I made polite conversation with him in the living room for a couple of minutes. I thanked him profusely for his understanding. I could see his eyes wander around the room a bit and his tone faltered, as if he was having trouble completing sentences while having other thoughts. "Um," he said, "uh… do you… do you happen to know where my bike is?" he asked. I paused, blank. "Bike?" I asked. It took me a moment, but yes. There had been a bike in the living room, hadn't there? Wheeeere was the bike? "You know, Nathan went to the store this morning, maybe he took the bike and locked it up outside, like at home, out of habit. I'll ask him when he's back," I said. Nathan was asleep in the bedroom, but I was trying to buy time to figure this out. "Ah, of course, sure, no worries," he said, having just given me $500 and consoled me for a loss I felt no grief about at all.

I went into the bedroom where Nathan was curled up on his side. I touched his shoulder gingerly and told him I was sorry to wake him but needed to ask him something. He rolled onto his back and sat up. I asked if he had taken Jake's bike to the store in the morning when he bought cigarettes. He confirmed that he had, but when I asked where it was now, he said he didn't know. I asked him if he'd left it at the store, if someone stole it, if he'd sold it. He just kept saying he didn't know, each time with greater exasperation, as if his answer should have satisfied me by now. I felt suspended behind the gate of decency preventing me from yelling at this man whose loss of a brother meant he definitely didn't care about a lost bike. At that moment, I noticed a plastic edge popping out from the pocket of Nathan's jeans, and grabbed at it without hesitation, but also without haste. I asked what it was, and he said, "That crystal meth thingy," with no remorse, or surprise. None. Like it was Tic Tacs or a receipt for nachos. I don't know how I was still surprised at this point, but I *was*. To me, crystal meth was the mythical mutant of all the street drugs, and meant losing your fucking mind, teeth, and girlfriend and maybe going into psychosis for a bit. I darted into the bathroom, expecting him to chase me, but he didn't flinch. I flushed it down the toilet and went to the trouble of washing out the bag before throwing it away. (My handling of this bag would be a source of extreme paranoia when they separated my suitcase for swatch testing at the airport; the fear of some infinitesimal amount of Nathan's drugs being found on my person while traveling has remained with me in the years since.)

I had more questions now: "Where did you get this? Is this what you were doing this morning? Have you been doing this for a while?" But Nathan went almost totally unresponsive — a short series of shrugs, closed eyes, hard swallows, and finally the barely audible request to please be left alone. It's hard to indulge in particular stereotypes about drugs. It makes you feel like an asshole — like you might just be putting evidence together based on sensationalized stories from an episode of *True Life* or *Intervention* to quell your paranoia and make yourself feel better, like you weren't the moron they took you for. But, based on his behavior, I pieced together that he'd been on the meth a couple days. He'd gone out for more while I was getting him a tube of Orajel at the Riteaid, which hadn't been for his wisdom teeth but probably for a mouth ulcer, which meth gives you. He'd smoked it in the shower so he could wait for the smell to filter out the window and wash it off his body. The porn and enhanced sex drive were also symptoms of the potent psychomotor stimulant.

I told him I needed to go and try to find this bike. It was still early in the day and about 85 degrees. My hope was that he actually had taken the bike to the store for cigarettes, and had then gone to pick up instead and returned on foot, too high to remember he'd left it. Magical thinking. It wasn't there. I went into a homeless encampment, set up in a small area of greenspace where Vermont meets Hollywood Boulevard, because it was not only littered with bikes but had a sort of maintenance area set up where people were inspecting chains and pumping tires surrounded by a bevy of wrenches. I don't know what I thought I was going to get there. I just thought: Bikes. *There* are some bikes.

A frail trans woman emerged from a tent with a cigarette between fingers with long unpolished fingernails filed to a point. She looked like she weighed about a pound for every year of her certain age, and she had no teeth but wore her hair like Diana Vreeland; I thought she was so, so beautiful. She called me "dear" and asked if she could help me. She spoke slowly and sweetly. I asked if she'd seen a silver bike, but I was really telling her I'd lost my will to live. She said, "My goodness, a silver bike?" almost like she was afraid of the idea. She wasn't aware of any silver bikes, but called some friends over, telling them to help this young lady. They wanted the whole story. They wanted to know why this very housed-looking woman was searching for a BMX bike made for doing tricks off dirt mounds and stuff. I sat on the concrete edge around a big flower bed filled with purple and yellow pansies, telling them about my boyfriend who had lost a bike while on crystal meth. They gave me some flack about liking bad boys and then some knowing sympathy. They told me it would be ok, and gave me the names of a couple bike shops they knew. One guy asked if I wanted to take him home. He said he'd kick my boyfriend's ass and he'd be good to me. I laughed, but then made the mistake of saying I had enough problems and didn't need to bring strange men home. I didn't actually mean to insinuate that he was strange. It felt like a turn of phrase that would have been taken as sarcasm, hyperbolic jest — *teasing* — in most other contexts. Well, he didn't like that, and it became clear that I was no longer welcome on the flower bench.

I made thirty calls to local bike shops at international rates, then gave up. Just as Nathan had always stood passively by, waiting for me to pay for things at the grocery store and camera shop and restaurants, he passively waited for me to fix this. I had to call Jake and tell him we didn't know where his bike was. I didn't mention the crystal meth; I blamed it on grief. I told him that Nathan had biked to the store early for cigarettes, and in his grief and fatigue he'd walked home and forgotten it there. Jake understood, but very calmly and rationally conveyed to me that it was a rare BMX bike, and that he'd had it for a long time — since he'd jumped off dirt mounds and stuff in his teens. It had both high monetary and sentimental value, and he would need to be compensated. I agreed wholeheartedly. I was so embarrassed. I felt worse for him than for Nathan. Nathan had only ever said horrible things about his brother, and I think his real sorrow was over the fact that there wouldn't be someone to compare himself to, to be better off than or not as bad as anymore. Instead, they'd say, "You're just like your brother. You'll end up just like your brother." I paid Jake the $500 we'd just gotten back as a rent refund for the missing bike, and to this day don't know what really happened to it. When I told another friend in recovery the story, he assured me Nathan had sold it for the drugs. He told me he had once stolen his mother's engagement ring and sold it for coke which was also a significant factor in his crashing his brother's car into a lamp post the same night. He got $75 for the ring. This wasn't a story I heard in Al-Anon, but I heard similar and much worse ones there every week. They never made me feel better.

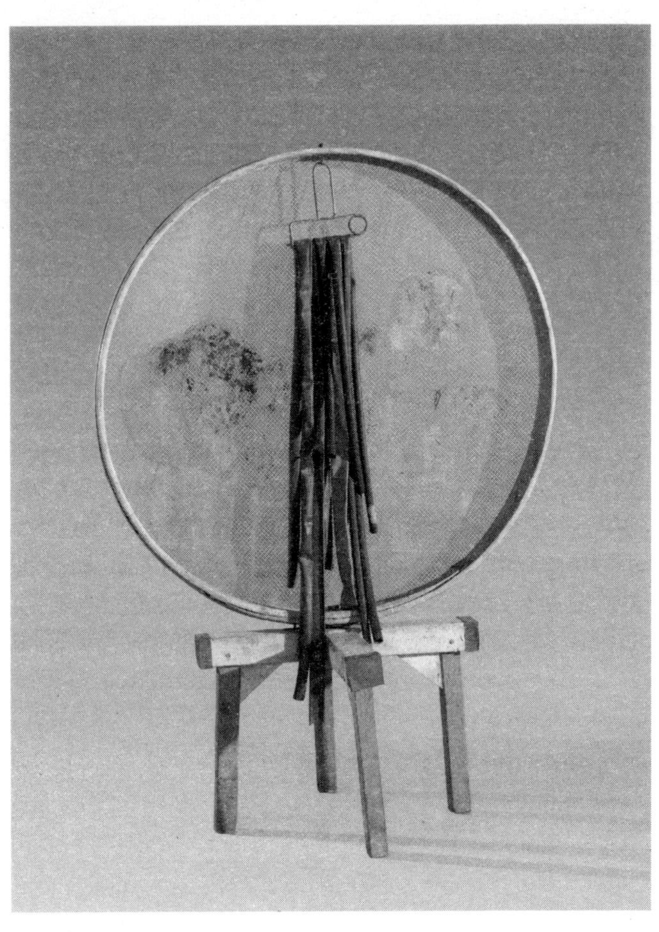

Figure 6

Untitled (Sortilegi), 1984

Carol Rama (1918–2015)

Wood, metal, tire tubes, and nail polish, Ursula Hauser Collection, Switzerland and © Archivio Carol Rama, Torino. Photo: Stefan Altenburger Photography Zürich

Fights and Flights

We got into a screaming match in the apartment the morning before we left, and barely made our flight back to England. I was slow to finish packing and cleaning, and he said I didn't care about him and didn't care if we missed the flight or Eric's funeral. All I cared about, he said, was cleaning Jake's kitchen. I screamed a looooong scream. No words, just spasm and piercing screech, rattling into a kind of staccato sob with the thrust of my convulsing diaphragm — a singer's strongest muscle. It had been building up. It was painful to reign in and painful to release. A shrill but somehow booming "HOW *FUCKING* DARE YOU" followed, and I recounted all the events from the last year to argue that it was him who didn't care and that I was still throwing everything I had at this doomed plague of a relationship. I pointed at him and watched the blood vessels bulge in my hands and arms. The delay caused by the cleaning and fighting and the failure to calculate the time needed to return the rental car meant we had to drive at 120 miles per hour toward the airport. I snaked chaotically between cars to gain the most minor lengths of ground. At one point, a pickup truck in front of me hit an old tire in the road, which caused the tailgate to pop open, and a massive iron wheelbarrow in the flatbed was thrust out onto the highway, just in front of me. I instinctively pulled the wheel to the right, and we narrowly escaped it crashing through the windshield, which would have caused a total loss of control.

By the time we got to our seats, we were sweaty and out of breath, and we redirected our fury at each other. We sat in silence all the way to England: on the thirteen-hour flight; on the three-hour train to his mother's town; in her car to the house. When we spoke to her, we did not look at each other. I don't think she noticed.

On the morning of the funeral, we met his father and stepmother in the parking lot of a hotel where we all got into a black car to follow the hearse. As we pulled into the cemetery, his stepmother let out a screeching cry that I saw ripple through her body, before she threw her face onto the shoulder of Nathan's father and wept. I am generally attracted to the beauty of dark things, but this was the only moment I found beautiful at that funeral. After the coffin was removed from the hearse, all followed the pallbearers in a parade of clashing hues. His mum told people to wear lots of color to the funeral because, she said, "he was a young lad." It was a disturbing calculus. From the pictures I'd seen of him, Eric was a fairly typical Gen X-er who wore band T-shirts and jeans and had the bad skin, and bloated face and belly of someone aged a decade beyond their years. The coroner's report specified that he died wearing crocs. I'm sorry, this just isn't a gem-tones type of guy. Her request that we camouflage the circumstances in summer colorways was an appeal for a personal favor. She wanted to see a palette of lemonade and beachballs honoring youth and dramatizing an unfair loss. In fact, it was a life pretty knowingly forfeited despite the efforts made by everyone here, except maybe me. I offered my complicity in a Barbie-pink midi-skirt purchased for the occasion in a part of the good grocery store that sells cotton clothes that don't last. I looked like an ugly tulip. After Nathan's father ended his testimony early because his efforts to dam his tears caused his throat to close, Richard's young wife sang a folk song in her native Russian. Even that wasn't as sad as it should be.

Eric's friend Richard was Richard D. James, Aphex Twin. He and Eric were friends, part of the same scene; they made the same kind of music, did the same drugs. Seeing him at this funeral was a staggering moment because I used to be around musicians of relative acclaim frequently. It was an excruciating reminder that I hadn't made anything in a year. I hadn't played a show in a year. I couldn't even remember the last time I'd listened to music. Perhaps I used Nathan as an excuse not to take care of myself, or as a project in which to envelop myself in order to avoid failing creatively. Perhaps I waded away from myself and abdicated the challenges of my ambitions for those of maintaining someone else's survival — someone who was reeeeallly bad at it, so there'd be plenty to do. I didn't want to give any more time to this. It was selfish thinking for a funeral, but I'd tried to think about Eric and couldn't connect. The fact was I didn't know him. I couldn't find empathy either. As far as I could tell, everyone in Nathan's family was not only horrible but miserable, and it made them awful to themselves and each other. Nathan had a million reasons for being the way he was, and I sympathized. But I didn't belong there.

Nathan drove his mother and me in her car to his father's house not far away, further out into the recesses of the country for the reception. Nathan's anger spilled out, abundant and uncontainable by a brain still processing LA street drugs, so he picked a fight with his mum, while driving, on the worst day of her life. He asked her what time Eric would have his first lager. "Was it before twelve? Would you make him wait 'til midday?" he asked. She was in shock or playing dumb, but either way Nathan got what he wanted. "What do you mean?"

she asked. She wore a mint-green top and pearls. He couldn't entertain this, but he shouldn't have started in the first place. Nathan laid into the accusations, pointing his finger forward in a stabbing rhythm, punctuating each point as he looked back at her through the rearview mirror. He went all the way back, starting with memories of being left alone as a teenager, and she started to cry and beg. "Stop, Nath! Stop, please stop! I can't, I can't," she pleaded.

But as is typical with stages of grief, she moved from denying his attacks to anger quickly. The muscle memory of adolescent discipline kicked in, and she commanded him to "Stop this AT ONCE! THIS INSTANT!" She leaned forward from the center of the car's back bench and brought her hands to the shoulder of each front seat. She was so irate she clamped her hands into fists and shook her head as she spoke, with spittle rocketing out as she gnawed into bad memories and turgid defenses. I folded my left arm across my chest and brought my right knuckles across my lips and slumped down, shut down. Their voices smothered each other's, and Nathan sped up on the single-lane country road flanked by high hedges, instinctually trying to get there faster and end this, but also seizing more control by producing greater fear in his passengers. A fifteen-foot-tall beast of a tractor from one of the nearby cattle farms appeared suddenly from around a curve, and we all screamed as Nathan veered left and slammed on the brakes. The car skidded side to side like we'd hit black ice. Our bodies flew forward and then crashed back against our seats as his mum's curdling wail crescendoed into the words "You are one NASTY, NASTY MAN!" He was no longer her son by that point. The absolutely fucking guttural sound of her accusation separated him from her permanently. He was her villain. Her curse.

No Safe Place

We left England only days after we got there, and went back to Marrakech. Nathan positioned grief as his reason for everything now, and that everything was a vacuous, energy-sucking nothing: he mostly slept; didn't want to talk or touch; he smoked out the window a lot. He wasn't using, but he was grief-stricken and absent again. I took a trip to London to get some of our things, and when I got back there was a woman's earring on my nightstand. Classic. How could it even be so classic? He apparently didn't have the energy to lie very well anymore. He just said he didn't know anything about it, didn't know where it came from. Like the bike — he didn't know. What else did I want? In retaliation I started texting ex-boyfriends. When I couldn't come up with a very good lie about who I was talking to, he spit a litany of insults at me armored with his elite pain. He knew I pitied him too much to defend myself.

He started getting up in the morning before me and just sitting there in the darkness. He started going out without saying anything. I found small splatters of blood on the bathroom floor and asked him if he was shooting heroin. He was sitting on the edge of the bed and he melted inward, brushed his hair away from his face, and held his palm to his cheek, eyes downcast. I threw some things in my suitcase and left. I prayed to God — who I didn't know I believed in — "Please don't let him follow me, please don't let him follow me." I said it softly, out loud. I was too afraid to look behind me as I dragged the suitcase down the dirt road of the medina, and I locked the door when I got into a taxi for the airport at the end of the street. He had never used there before. There were no more safe places.

I stayed with friends in London until the subletter's rental period at the flat was over. First there were long apologies from Nathan via text and email, then just dejected bitterness. My responses varied. For the most part I told him I loved him and he needed to go to rehab, but sometimes I said mean things — about the crashed car and meth and crack and all that money. He came back to London and stayed at the vacant Notting Hill apartment of a friend in recovery who had some money. I think he usually used it as a rental, but Nathan probably had an easy time convincing him to let him stay there, especially if he had promised it would just be a couple nights, which I'm sure he did: "My brother died. I relapsed. My girlfriend left me. My mother hates me. I have no money and nowhere to stay." I knew he was using now, because his correspondence was just too manic, totally unhinged — self-grasping and self-pitying and filled with obscene accusations — pages and pages. Then I'd get a text asking what the Netflix password was. Somehow he managed to effectively abide by a schedule we established for which one of us would stay at the flat on particular nights of the week until the lease was up. When he was in his addiction, he was awful: entitled, petty, whiny, a liar, manipulative. But I didn't feel physically unsafe. I didn't think he would just let himself into the flat on one of my nights. But he wasn't done with me.

I wish I'd been asleep. I could have been. It was about 10:30 at night, a weekday, and I was watching something stupid in bed on my computer. I heard something being jammed under the door; the crinkling of paper searching for a little extra width where the wood might've been unevenly planed. Then there was a little whoosh across the floor as the parcel was given a final push from the outside. I didn't move. That's just not what you want. When you know you have a rancorous, small, small man of an ex-boyfriend who also may or may not be totally lucid due to the co-morbidities of grief and addiction, a letter under your door at 10:30 just really is not what you want.

It promised the worst. It promised to love me forever. It promised I had been the love of his life. It promised he was sorry. It promised it was all just his disease. He said he couldn't live like this and was going to the garage to take care of things and hoped it would protect the people he loved. I made the quick decision not to call for help because it would take too long for someone to arrive; this letter promised a pretty limited window in which to act. I also figured that despite being in whatever kind of state he was in, he wanted me to know because he wanted me to stop him. I worried anybody else might freak him out and make him do something stupid; getting to the door of the garage at the bottom of the stairwell, it felt like maybe that was a misjudgment. I was alone in the only part of the building without phone reception, and no one would hear me if I screamed for help. I looked through the small window on the door to the garage and nearly all the parking places were taken. There wouldn't be too many people coming home at this hour. I looked for Nathan, but there were too many dark recesses, despite the oppressively bright, putrid yellow, fluorescent lights. The available exit strategies also weren't ideal. You had to put in a six-digit code on a security pad to enter and exit the garage. This might take time I didn't have on the other side of the door. Alternatively, I could run across the garage and press a button on the large door to the street if I needed to, but it was slow to open as all the gears and rods fit into geometric alignment. Visions flashed of Nathan writhing on a rope, savable; passed out from an overdose, savable; or letting out the blood from his wrists, savable. I pressed the code into the interior security panel and slowly pushed the door open just enough to yell out into the space. "Hello? Hello? Nathan?" I said the door code numbers to myself softly. The code to come back in was different and I really didn't know if I had it right. I inched forward, staying close to the now open door like it was a shield. This all felt wrong now, but underground garages sort of feel like that anyway, so I advanced. The door closed behind me and my vision darted around the garage, worried this was a trap and that I had come down here because part of me wanted it all over for us. I went to the center of the garage and rotated my body around, slowly, saying his name and feeling the horrible feeling you get when you see someone behind the final girl in a horror movie. I held still and quiet, hoping I would hear movement. I didn't even realize I was holding my breath, and when I finally inhaled, I took two rapid heavy, deep, uncontrolled breaths and felt the warm wetness in my eye. If he was there, he hadn't actually wanted to be found and couldn't be helped. If he wasn't there, he had put me through another unforgiveable rehearsal of his permanent loss.

When I got back to the flat I was again careful. Maybe he saw me leave and came in while I was down there. No. I had reception back and texted him to please let me know if he was ok; that I had read the letter and gone to the garage but no one was there and I was not ok at all. He texted back, "Good."

My Girls

I felt neither safe nor sane and went to my aunt's house in Somerset for the weekend to hide. I was floating, blank, still in shock. Writing out those memories still makes me feel dizzy and off. But I was hoping that seeing some art would make me feel better. Not far from where she lives, Hauser and Wirth have a large art gallery with multiple viewing rooms. They converted the structure from an eighteenth-century barn. Behind the galleries is a 1.5-acre perennial meadow created by landscape designer Piet Oudolf, who also designed the gardens along the High Line Park in New York. This felt familiar. I read the names of some of the species planted in the meadow, and said them aloud as though they might have a taste: Sesleria autumnalis (a vibrant green grass), Cimicifuga brunette (a dark-chocolate-colored foliage with some deep purple hues), Gillenia trifoliate (a flowering plant with red stems and three-lobed leaves with airy sprays of star-shaped flowers, white as picket fences), and Astrantia "Venice" (booming big fuchsia blooms with a dazzling geometry of tiered petals), among others.

Spread across the viewing rooms was an exhibition of works by female artists from the private collection of Ursula Hauser, who founded the gallery with her daughter and son-in-law in 1992. In the previous year I'd started having the kind of encounters with individual works of art that I've described, which both gave shape to the awfulness of my experiences and momentarily remedied them by offering a calm of sheer acknowledgement and shared sentiment. What I walked into was an extensive and overwhelming collection of works, many by artists I didn't know, which personified the lexicon of my year: exhaustion, failure, collapse, hanging, mess, melt, decay, hallucination, illness, disease, pallor, skin, pornography, raw, poison, death. There was even a drawing of a cyclops by Méret Oppenheim — *Der verliebte Polyphem (The enamored Polyphem)*, in oil crayon on paper, from 1973. There were works by old friends: Louise Bourgeois, Oppenheim, and my Eva. I did not know the work of Alina Szapocznikow or Carol Rama before seeing it there, but I found theirs the most resonant among the works, and have since appraised them as further evidence of the effective approach to care offered by the autobiographical sculpting of the body. With every room I passed through I felt like I was having some different part of me bandaged up in gauze.

From Szapocznikow, I learned the practice of reimagining bad things in some aesthetic way that affords agency and some protective distance. In post-war Communist Poland, she was commissioned by the government to design large monuments. She departed from these political and prescriptive memorial works when she moved to Paris in 1963 (after first living there from 1948–51 among a Polish expat community).[75] She immersed herself in an artistic social circle of the Nouveau Realists, helmed by art critic Pierre Restany. In Paris, she developed a distinctly more personal and experimental practice, typified by sensualized body parts and unnatural colors. She also made a series of sculpted tumors, desserts, phallic lamps, and photographs of chewed gum. In many of these series, the commemorative approach once taken with national memorials seems to have been re-directed toward her own life.

The anatomy of Szapocznikow's work is figurative, but fragmented and manipulated. Her work has often been read as a record of her traumatic experiences during the holocaust, and of her having breast cancer, which she was diagnosed with in 1969. She received a mastectomy in 1972, and died in 1973 at the age of forty-six, at which point the cancer had spread to her bones. She did not make these experiences nicer; she undermined the power they exerted over her by making them hers, and weirder. In *Tear* (1971) (Figure 3), a molded polyester breast with a clear pink, jelly-like nipple both hangs on and emerges from a discolored white fabric mounted to a backing board made stiff by a splattering of the same polyester from which the breast is made. The fabric is described as "fleece" in the list of materials, but has the perforations and texture of lace. It looks like a tablecloth gathered up at the end of an evening dinner where tapered candles dripped freely down and wine was spilled. It also looks like a cum rag. It's messy, wet looking, and riddled with a wry duality. The title encourages us to see sadness associated with crying, but this breast could also be protruding from the folds of bedclothes. Perhaps we are meant to see "tear," as in "pull apart," "rip in two," "shred" — something active and provoked by the impatience before a sexual encounter.

Referring to work like *Dessert III* (1971), composed of hot-pink breasts with bright yellow nipples displayed on a white porcelain cake stand, feminist art historian Griselda Pollock has said, "Before she underwent a mastectomy, she made casts of scrumptious breasts that float free and replicate, sometimes accumulating like piles of candy, offering a non-maternal and non-eroticized appeal to the oral."[76] Through aesthetic strategies she reimagines the site of her disease as colorful, vital, sweet. This is not the kind of care sought by Nengudi, whose attention to healing suggests a belief that care will resolve the condition. Szapocznikow's work seems to attempt to preserve and externalize what proved to be a terminal illness where it can be controlled, importantly by making it an object aestheticized in signature ways. This is echoed by Szapocznikow, who said, "I produce awkward objects. This absurd and convulsive mania proves the existence of an unknown, secret gland, necessary for life… I want to exalt the ephemeral in the folds of our body… Through casts of the body I try to fix the fleeting moments of life…"[77] I take her "convulsive mania" to be her compulsive production of art, which she defines as a secret gland that is both necessary to live and proof of our existence, or that one has lived. By her own rationale, art kept her alive, and it exists now as a document of that life.

Her work *Stela (Stèle)* (1968) (Figure 4) is the one that most directly informed my verbalization of the Death Melt, even though it existed first as an affective anomaly experienced in front of *Seven Poles*. Presented on a short white platform under a rectangular glass case, the tall sculpture rose to the middle of my stomach. The title references funeral monuments, but it is unclear whether the woman depicted in it is alive or dead. She appears in between; submerged in a black liquid, not gone yet but also not sure to survive. Her nose, mouth, and knees protrude from the polyester resin and polyurethane foam — materials also used by Hesse to present a sense of wetness. Here they look like tar: thick, bubbling, and toxic. Some of the black material is spread across her lips, compounding its haunting effect. Another in-between, sexual and deathly gesture, its color suggests poison or a "kiss of death" but the placement hints at lipstick, messily smeared in passion. It drips in a perfect tear shape at the edge, giving it a slow sense of movement, but it's unclear whether this liquid has come from inside or outside her body. Neither seem particularly preferable.

Szapocznikow's sculptures took up much of the first room of the exhibition, while the next room was dominated by Rama's work. These felt less rooted in appropriative fantasy than in confrontation, albeit visually abstract. Honesty and confession were conveyed through tactility and rawness. Influenced by Rama, I've sought to correct the silence and secrecy I maintained throughout my relationship with Nathan, and to be as explicit as Rama was about her use of her work as a practice of care. She has said, "We all have our own tropical diseases within us, for which we seek a remedy. My remedy is painting."[78] For her, then, care was often provided in the same kind of sexual wetness that Hesse and Szapocznikow explored and utilized, but perhaps even more explicitly *splattered*. For Rama, care might be read as orgasmic, or perhaps extatically violent. *Bricolage* (1964) (Figure 5) was a work in the exhibition that demonstrated this. It was part of a series of the same name (comprising mostly variations of the splatter), which she worked on throughout the 1960s, and which fused organic and inorganic material.[79] The splatter in the exhibition's *Bricolage* work looked like hardened, shiny glue, but was dotted with the tiny circles and craters that looked like the domes of gas that appear when a pancake is ready to flip. It conflated all things expelled suddenly or uncontrollably from the body: vomit, semen, or blood sprayed against the wall due to an attack. It's unclear what the substance actually was; only "mixed media" was listed under materials. This bubbling, dripping brown stain, laid against a bright red background was representative of a wider oeuvre, started in the mid-1930s, which celebrated other sexual and bodily themes, or what author Sarah Lehrer-Graiwer described as "over-sexed, vulgar, dirty, and disfigured bodies" which "roiled propriety and uptight norms, directly challenging the far-right national politics of the day."[80]

Indeed, Rama's first exhibition at Faber gallery in Turin was censored as "obscene" by the Italian Fascist government in 1945, and it is believed that works were not only withdrawn, but that some were also destroyed.[81] Throughout her career, her sexual and explicit, sometimes grotesque representations were problematized and pathologized. In his text "The Phantom Limb: Carol Rama and the History of Art" (2015), theorist Paul B. Preciado asserts that "the image of Carol Rama oscillates between the cultural tropes of the perverted child, the lesbian, the monster, the woman-without-children, the nymphomaniac, the old witch"[82] and has been historicized as "pornographic, mentally ill, fetishized, and sexually deviant."[83] To be clear: I do not seek to pathologize Rama's sexuality, sexual representations, or other confrontational work. As products of the artistic practice she identifies as her method of care and "remedy," I assert instead that they are what kept her well.

The Rama I was most drawn to was *Untitled (Sortilegi)* (1984) (Figure 6). She draped rosy and bruise-colored deflated rubber tubes over a little metal hook hung from a large, circular, wooden frame, which had mesh stretched across it. The accumulated lengths of rubber looked like dry old guts. The exhibition catalog corroborated that her use of provocative, morbid aesthetics had an autobiographical element. They claimed the rubber tubes made direct reference to her father, who committed suicide when his bicycle company went bankrupt, and compared the tubes to machine parts, human skin, and loose appendages.[84] Within the mesh were areas of nail polish in more violent hues, like it had been strained through or thrown there, further echoing a sense of loss and violence, or violent loss. The abject quality of the tubes offers a kind of confrontation with death or grief that is supported by the title as well. "Sortilegi" translates as "spells" — the kind related to sorcery or witchcraft. The use of a material so closely related to her dead father becomes spectral within a context that abides by its own metaphysical logics. Importantly, spells actively pursue results. We may not know what Rama requested, processed, or pursued with this work, but the title suggests she sought a specific outcome in the same way more traditional forms of care do.

In the final viewing room were the Hesse works. I have spoken about my encounter with her art as a therapeutic experience. I also believe exploring aesthetic markers of bodily pleasure, arousal, and sensitivity in the face of physical and emotional distress was Hesse's way of retaining personal agency and autonomy, particularly while she was under medical care. This book has made a limited exploration of sexuality, which I consider an important, signifying lack. In other words, the absence of pleasure is so glaring it highlights the need to recover it. My attraction to the sexual substances in Hesse's work was a reminder of the importance of sex and physical connection to me, which is inherently linked to my physical and mental health. I believe it was for Hesse too, which a comparison of her work at the exhibition with some of later pieces effectively evidences.

The back gallery of the exhibition had two of what I consider to be Hesse's most important works. These "in-betweens" mark her shift from painting to sculpture. They are more paintings than sculptures in that they hang on the wall, but they have areas of sculptural relief and little sculptural antennas popping off of them. They are not Death Melty, but bright, erectile, sort of horny little works, which precede her more mature sexual aesthetic explorations. *Oomamaboomba* (1965) (Figure 7) has a light-blue, almost seafoam-colored background. An abstract, lemon-lime shape takes up most of the canvas, with three narrow, raised sections at the top — the shape of kazoos or ladyfingers. A sort of collar with thin black and white lines separates these shapes from the larger, main triangular space. Two actual rods jut out from the canvas, both wrapped in cord. The larger one swoops down to the left and spirals from a bright, deep lavender to progressively diluted shades of hot pink until it becomes pastel.

H + H (1965) has a similar antenna emerging from a pearl-colored, cervical-shaped piece of wood mounted to the top of the canvas, and which is re-connected into one of two pale, orangey-tan ovary-like shapes. These works are without a sense of wetness and bodily fluid, despite their shapes reminiscent of female anatomy and perky sense of arousal. The shift from exploring the body in these early works to later embracing the explicit artifacts of orgasm further chimes with some of Hesse's medical history, which positioned her sexuality and sexual health as something she took care in cultivating and maintaining. Given the evidence that her later work was an extension of her care, I read these early works in a similar way.

In one of her diary passages from 1958, before contraceptive pills were made available, Hesse expressed "extreme fear" at possibility of her work and professional progress being not only halted but undone, fear of her life being fundamentally redirected. She did not say that she was fearful of being pregnant, but in an entry six days later she explained that she "survived through a week or more of torment and worry of a most serious nature" due to "the fact that [she] was 9 days late with [her] period after a major accident with protective paraphernalia right at the time of ovulation."[85] Hesse relays the common fear of motherhood rendering the planned trajectory of one's life permanently irretrievable, and this seems to be cause of the "extreme fear" mentioned in the earlier entry. At other points in the diary, Hesse does express wanting to have children, but this desire is always set at a distance, in a future she assumed responsibility for designing and planning.

A year later she said, "I wish I could fulfill my sensual and sexual desires without being involved with the person."[86] In the same entry, she goes on to express dissatisfaction with men with whom she had had relationships, and refers to sexual problems, feelings of restlessness and dissatisfaction, and wanting to be with a more mature, "worldly partner."[87] These entries confirm that Hesse was sexually active, using methods of birth control, and even aware of when she was ovulating. She emphasized her enjoyment of sex, but framed relationships as disappointing, yet necessary for her access to it; rather than a priority in pursuit of marriage or having a family. The passages above evidence the importance of sex and career to Hesse, and position birth control as what accommodated both.

Her juicier, more playfully genital sculptural objects emerged at the same time as some of the most radical medical interventions being made at the site of the female body, which were also key to the momentum and success of the second feminist wave, ensuring reproductive rights, which fundamentally changed the experience of female embodiment and the conditions under which one's life and identity could be forged. These advances are particularly important to consider given that most countries where the artists explored in this book are from legalized access to oral contraceptive pills or abortion within about ten years of one another, evidencing that reproductive activism was a concentrated and intercontinental movement — perhaps at the core of a global shift in how female artists represented and related to the body. The United States introduced birth control pills in 1960 and a re-designed IUD in 1964 that were both nearly one hundred percent effective.[88] The UK made the pill available to married women in 1961, and in 1967 they legalized its use by unmarried women, and also legalized abortion.[89] The US legalized abortion in 1973 following the watershed trial, Roe vs Wade, though this was overturned in 2022, leaving access to be determined at state level.[90] The pill arrived in Italy in 1964, but was prohibited from being sold in pharmacies until 1970. Abortion was legalized in Italy in 1978.[91] However, women's relationships to these treatments were strongly differentiated by race; Black and indigenous women who were forcibly sterilized in the US sometimes appraised the availability of contraception and abortion negatively.[92]

Importantly, there are also ties between the Pill—a medication made more widely available largely due to feminist activism — and the wider development of hormone-based treatments. For example, it was discovered that breast cancer responded to hormonal treatments by accident in 1972, during trials of a new emergency contraceptive: the "morning after" pill. This culminated in the production of Tamoxifen — a pill-based treatment that was crucially less invasive than surgery or radiation, and still one of the most widely used breast cancer treatments today.[93]

Hesse's diaries suggest an awareness of these shifts based on how she relates to sex and her body in the diaries before oral contraceptives were available as compared to after she starts taking them, which there is evidence of in the diaries. She frequently kept lists of things to do or procure. On a Friday in July of 1966, Hesse listed "Demotil and Orthonovun" [*sic*] at the bottom of her entry for the day — presumably two medications she needed to obtain.[94] Ortho-novum was a common birth control pill at the time of Hesse's writing. It was released in the United States in 1963, only the second oral contraceptive to come to market.[95] Six months later, on January 1, 1967 she wrote:

> I have a new journal in which I will attempt to write
> daily. Sol's present
>
> I met a man I can like
> Even a second man I like
>
> I am beginning to find my anger against Doyle
> I have taken my wedding ring off
> I take my woman pills
> I am working well and eager to go on.
> Might even be ready for 1st one man by next fall.[96]

I've maintained the stylization of the text as it appears in the diary because it contributes to the pointed tone and measured pace of these provocative declarations. There are several elements to this passage that resonate with a pro-sex feminist self-possession, and a rejection of monogamy, which starkly contrast the fear conveyed in earlier passages around both faulty forms of birth control and the frustration of pursuing relationships to access sex. This interpretation rests upon my reading of "woman pills" as how Hesse describes the Pill. The appearance of Ortho-novum in her diary before this entry evidences this, as does a statement made earlier in 1966 where she said, "I must go to Dr. to become woman, to allow myself to be woman when I want to. Shit, I am 30+ I have a right to have sex if I want."[97] Given that the statement concludes with the use of her age to justify her desire for sex, this colors the use of "woman" in the previous lines as a marker of maturity, and thus having a sexual life and identity. In this context, going to the doctor to "allow [herself] to be a woman" suggests securing birth control, which is then mentioned later in the diary. The term "woman pills" can thus be linked back to this entry where she conflates womanhood with sexual activity, which must be accommodated or controlled at the medical level.

The passage is written with a bold confidence that starkly contrasts with the fear laden in an earlier passage in which she thinks she might be pregnant and laments the failure of contraception. By liking two men she expresses a rejection of the earlier norms she alluded to whereby she pursued monogamous relationships in order to access sex. An increased sense of independence and self-possession are further suggested by finding anger against "Doyle," her ex-husband Tom Doyle, and her removal of her wedding ring — both positioned by her as new and revelatory. Moreover, actions and revelations seem to provide her with the confidence she requires to pursue her first solo show, which she also defined in the passage above in masculine terms. I argue her use of birth control directly contributed to her sense of self-possession and a pursuit of sex without fear of pregnancy or obligation to commit to a relationship, which resulted in Hesse's work becoming more sexually provocative and experimental.

Again, whereas *Oomamaboomba* and *H + H* were both done in 1965, by 1966 — at which point I argue she was being prescribed oral contraceptives — Hesse was experimenting with materials with heavily sexual connotations such as rubber, latex, and plastics, which drew associations to condoms, diaphragms, sex toys, and fetish wear; while the shiny, fluid-like aesthetics of their surfaces further recalled substances used, or secreted during sexual encounters, such as lubricants, spermicides, semen, vaginal fluid, saliva, and sweat. This was compounded by the anatomical shapes and neutral flesh tones she sculpted them in. Examples included *Untitled* (1966) — made of enamel, papier-mâché, and rubber — which comprised two forms dangling from a string nailed to a high point on the wall. One was a long, thin phallic shape, and the other looked testicular. *Total Zero* (1966), also made of rubber, acrylic, and polyurethane, was a black shiny inner-tube shape, with a small rod jutting out from it like a sperm trying to penetrate the cervix. *Schema* (1967) was made of a glistening brown latex, and looked like the thirty-day blister packs that birth control pills are packaged in. These highly erotic, graphic aesthetics were pursued through to the production of *Seven Poles,* whose slippery sexual surface was discussed earlier.

That day, the work of Szapocznikow, Rama, and Hesse demonstrated a variety of remedial strategies, which might be adapted in myriad forms: appropriative fantasy, confrontational honesty, and autonomous sensuality. Despite feeling like I was drowning in the tar of Szapocznikow's *St è le,* I imagined Hesse's *Seven Poles* grabbing my body and pushing it into a future where I could be a hot-pink and lavender erection springing out into space.

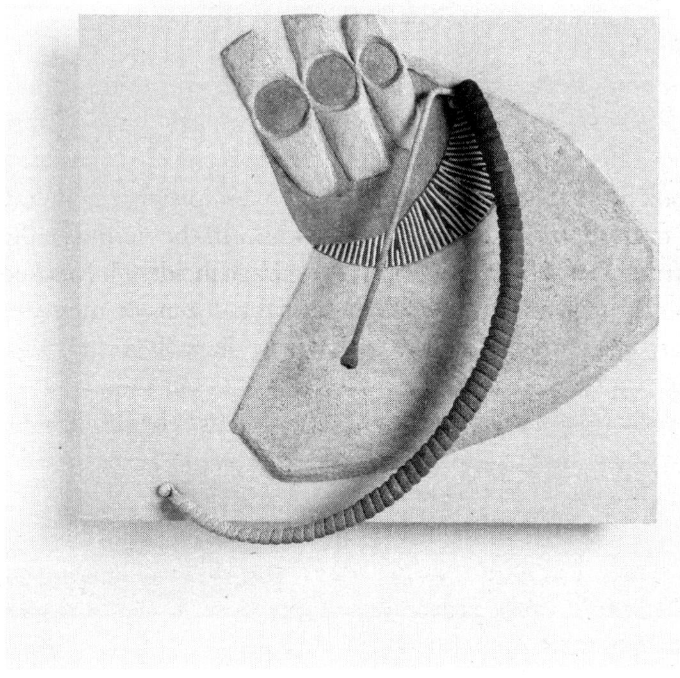

Figure 7

Oomamaboomba, 1965

Eva Hesse (1936–1970)

Tempera, enamel, rope, cord, metal, modeling compound (glue plaster, wood-shavings), particle board, wood

Ursula Hauser Collection, Switzerland and © The Estate of Eva Hesse

Courtesy Hauser & Wirth

Photo: Abby Robinson

The End

It took me another year to get Nathan completely out of my life, even though the last time I saw him in the flesh was the morning I left Marrakech. After the garage incident he hacked into my email and forwarded himself the dozens of messages in my drafts folder that I used as my diary. I never spoke of using that account as a diary to him or anyone. I did so precisely because diaries are things prone to being read when left around. I thought my thoughts were safe there. I don't know what he went looking for, but what he found was a truly desperate record, less a diary than an impressionistic glossary on the special subject of my spiraling decline: fragments of sentences, words repeated in columns, all to the effect of needing rescue, feeling dead, blankness, not knowing what to do. There was a lot of frustration over the resolve that I *did* miss him but could not understand this in any logical terms. In a way, I was glad he found them, because they were proof that he had made me so very obviously unwell. Long emails went back and forth for about a week, and I kept insisting he needed treatment and that too many lines had been crossed to ever consider being together again. Finally, he told me he had been accepted into a reputable rehab facility, Clouds House, in Wiltshire. He would be there eight weeks, and use of a phone was prohibited. No text messages in the middle of the night, no suicide notes under the door. I counted down the days until he left.

I started investigating other remedies, too. I was trying to practice the kind of "self-care" that was being promoted everywhere at the time, but which has since been largely debunked; rejected (conceptually, at least) for how it degrades community care in prioritization of individualized notions of resilience, wellness, and self-improvement, accessed through products and services which make care a costly, often cosmetic routine.[98] Getting my nails done became a monthly indulgence. My face masks with placenta did nothing for my mood, but my skin never looked better.

I made more time for exhibitions, but they didn't all have the same effects as sculptures did. When I attended a London show of works inspired by Stanley Kubrick, there was a small Impressionist-style painting in the entryway which stood out among the rest of the more contemporary-looking works and installations. It was by Kubrick's widow, Christiane, whose paintings were often used to fill the walls in his films' interior shots. The apartment belonging to Tom Cruise and Nicole Kidman's characters in *Eyes Wide Shut* is positively littered with them. I looked her up and found out that she taught painting classes about an hour away from London, in the former barn of her manor house in St. Albans. It felt fitting to try to regain my creative energy by studying under a woman whose practice was quite literally placed in the background of her husband's own immense artistic worlds.

In the class I took from her, objects were assembled in front of me to be copied, made into a still-life painting. Colorful flowers from her garden were set beside old green bottles and blue vases on pale pine stools. I looked for the point where the light hit them and used dashes of titanium white to mark these spots. After hours of staring at the same thing and neither particularly effectively nor gleefully replicating these objects in oil paint, my focus would drift, and different images surfaced from the grief that painting was meant to distract me from. I imagined him as a large dog with short hair and black eyes, underfed and snarling. I fixated on the top of the canine tooth in his lower jaw, the left one. I thought about adding the white to mark its point, or just slathering it in tomato red, trying simultaneously to make something beautiful and take control of the pain I found it hard to articulate but easy to re-cast in images that were violent but pedestrian. The red would obviously insinuate blood. I'll leave the wound's location to your imagination because it's a metaphor anyway. What would hurt the most? So painting didn't work. Because of a simple admin error, I did accidentally get invited to the Kubrick family Christmas party that year though, and it was a BALL.

I felt better when I wrote, shared the writing, and hauled my editor to Somerset to see the Hauser and Wirth show and pitch him the idea for this book. I have presented variations and sections of this text at conferences, in seminars, at research days, and to my friends. I know there are some shifts in tone and that some academic residue is left on parts of it. I enjoy and embrace the trail of slime that betrays where these ideas have been and how they got here because it has involved an intensely collaborative, supportive, creative process full of care and connection. It's sticky. I encourage a writing of the self in one's own terms, but know that we live interdependently. That said, some relationships just require a loving detachment, and their end might necessitate a tiny drop of the retail therapy we know is bad.

On the day of Nathan's departure for rehab, I sent one last email wishing him well. It was measured and heartfelt, and took account of what we'd been through together and extended deep and true wishes and hopes for him to get well. He wrote back that he'd missed his train and asked if I could put some money in his account to buy another ticket, and could I do it quickly, because there was only one more train that would get him in during check-in hours. Before writing this section, I made myself a Campari and soda and some chocolate mousse. My breathing was shallow and a bit huffy. I can still feel tension and heat around my sternum, and I've made a plan to reward myself with new jewelry when it's done. It's almost done.

More than any other moment in this sordid tale, this one is the hardest to write about because it felt like the most unfair test. I guess I should have said, "No, Nathan. I know you wanted to get high one last time before rehab and either spent the train money on drugs or missed it because you were strung out." But then he'd still be in London. The texts, the letters, the emails would all come back, and maybe he'd even get clean long enough to convince me to give it just one more try. If I wanted a future free of this man, I had to pay for it. I also had to sprint. It was Saturday and the bank closed early. I was low on cash and had to deposit a check in my account before they closed in order to be able to send Nathan the money. I remember crying as I ran on Mare street, a busy commercial road with tons of foot traffic, narrow pavements, and the particular chaos that comes from fostering too many bus routes. It's an area thick with white noise and people waiting in clusters to become passengers. I felt rich disdain for everyone I nearly collided with over the half mile distance to the bank. They were between me and myself. Thrashing them to the ground would be worth my survival. I have never run like this. My lungs were burning, my chest was heaving, my face was wet. When I got to the bank, I quivered like I'd just come in from a hailstorm, and the tops of my ears stung. I kept my eyes down as I slid the signed check over to the teller to deposit, my fingertips fluttering like the needle of a seismograph. To confirm the account she said my name like a question. I guess I was still there. I completed the transfer on my phone outside and texted Nathan to confirm he'd received it. Then he asked if I could send another fifty because the price had gone up. Fuck it. I did; £37 left for me. I leaned back against the cold, stone, Neo-classical building in which the bank operated and slid down its facade and wept until the light of the day changed. The messages stopped, but *Seven Poles* still looks the same.

Do you know the jewelry designer Tessa Metcalfe? She makes beautiful rings.

Endnotes

1 Trends and Geographic Patterns and Synthetic Opioid Overdose Deaths – United States, 2013-2019. *Morbidity and Mortality Weekly Report*, Vol. 70, No 6. Available at: https://www.cdc.gov/mmwr/volumes/70/wr/mm7006a4.htm?s_cid=mm7006a4_w
2 Laurent Fournier, *Autotheory as Feminist Practice in Art, Writing, and Criticism* (London: The MIT Press, 2022), p. 7.
3 Ibid., p. 8
4 Ibid., p. 3
5 Ibid., p. 7.
6 Hiʻilei Julia Kawehipuaakahaopulani Hobart and Tamara Kneese, "Radical Care: Survival Strategies for Uncertain Times," 2020, p. 2. Available at https://uwethicsofcare.gws.wisc.edu/wpcontent/uploads/2020/04/Hobart-and-Tamara-Kneese-2020.pdf
7 The Care Collective (Andreas Chatzidakis, Jamie Hakim, Jo Littler, Catherine Rottenberg, and Lynne Segal), *The Care Manifesto: The Politics of Interdependence* (London: Verso, 2020), p. 4.
8 Michel Foucault, Luther H. Martin, Huck Gutman, and Patrick H. Hutton, *Technologies of the Self: A Seminar with Michel Foucault* (Amherst: University of Massachusetts Press, 1988), p. 20.
9 Ibid., p. 27.
10 Ibid.
11 Holland Cotter, "Agnes Martin," *Art Journal* 57, no. 3, 1998, pp. 77–80. Available at https://doi.org/10.2307/777974.

12 Ibid.
13 Ela Przybyło, "Ace and aro lesbian art and theory with Agnes Martin and Yayoi Kusama," *Journal of Lesbian Studies*, 26(1), 2022, pp. 89–112. Available at https://doi.org/10.1080/10894160.2021.1958732
14 Agnes Martin, quoted in Ann Wilson, "Linear Webs," *Art & Artists* 1, October 1966, p. 48.
15 https://www.youtube.com/watch?v=GmgERKy210o
16 Carolee Schneemann, *Imaging Her Erotics: Essays, Interviews, Projects* (Cambridge Massachusetts and London: The MIT Press, 2002), p. 319.
17 Bruce R. McPherson (ed.), Carolee Schneemann, *More Than Meat Joy: Performance Works and Selected Writings* (New York: McPherson & Company, 1997).
18 Stuart Hall, 'Black Diaspora Artists in Britain: Three 'Moments' in Post- War History', *History Workshop Journal*, 61: 1, Spring 2006, 18.
19 https://www.thetimes.com/culture/books/article/sarah-lucas-im-60-life-isnt-over-bjxlfqnxq
20 Ibid.
21 Lucy Lippard. *Eva Hesse,* (New York: New York University Press, 1976), p. 13.
22 Ibid.
23 Eva Hesse and Barry Rosen with assistance from Tamara Bloomberg (eds.), *Diaries*. (New Haven: Yale University Press in association with Hauser & Wirth, 2016), p. 315.
24 Mi-Kyung Yun et al., "Catalysis and Sulfa Drug Resistance in Dihydropteroate Synthase," *Science*, Vol. 335, no. 6072, March 2, 2012, pp. 1110–1114.
25 Eva Hesse diary entry, July 14, 1966, Oberlin 1977.52.29, Eva Hesse Archive, Allen Memorial Art Museum, Oberlin College, Oberlin, Ohio; Eva Hesse papers, 1914–1970, bulk 1960–1970 dates. Archives of American Art, Smith-

sonian Institution.

26 Bernard Do et al., "Sensitive Quantification of Diphemanil Methyl Sulphate in Human Plasma by Liquid Chromatography–tandem Mass Spectrometry," *Journal of Chromatography*, vol. 845, issue 1, 2007, pp. 104–108.

27 Eva Hesse diary entry, April 9, 1965, Oberlin 1977.52.27, Eva Hesse Archive, Allen Memorial Art Museum, Oberlin College, Oberlin, Ohio; Eva Hesse papers, 1914–1970, bulk 1960–1970 dates. Archives of American Art, Smithsonian Institution.

28 Andrew M. Colman, "Chlordiazepoxide," *A Dictionary of Psychology* (Oxford: Oxford University Press, 2015). Available at https://www-oxfordreference-com.sussex.idm.oclc.org/view/10.1093/acref/9780199657681.001.0001/acref-9780199657681-e-1437

29 Eva Hesse diary entry, May 1, 1962, Oberlin 1977.52.58.28-44 AND 1977.52.76.57, Eva Hesse Archive, Allen Memorial Art Museum, Oberlin College, Oberlin, Ohio; Eva Hesse papers, 1914–1970, bulk 1960–1970 dates. Archives of American Art, Smithsonian Institution.

30 Eva Hesse, *Diaries,* p. 382.

31 Eva Hesse diary entry, January 4, 1967, Oberlin 1977.52.41, Eva Hesse Archive, Allen Memorial Art Museum, Oberlin College, Oberlin, Ohio; Eva Hesse papers, 1914–1970, bulk 1960–1970 dates. Archives of American Art, Smithsonian Institution.

32 Lucy Lippard, *Eva Hesse* (New York: Da Capo Press, 1992), p. 218.

33 Eva Hesse, *Diaries*, p. 228.

34 Eva Hesse diary entry, January 21, 1959, Oberlin 1977.52.40, Eva Hesse Archive, Allen Memorial Art Museum, Oberlin College, Oberlin, Ohio; Eva Hesse papers, 1914–1970, bulk 1960–1970 dates. Archives of American

Art, Smithsonian Institution.

35 Eva Hesse, *Diaries*, p. 884.

36 Lucy Lippard, *Eva Hesse*, p. 220.

37 LIbid., p. 161.

38 Ibid., p. 160.

39 Ibid., p. 155.

40 Eva Hesse, *Diaries*, p. 884.

41 Hesse, Eva, and Cindy Nemser, *Eva Hesse*. Edited by Mignon Nixon (Cambridge, Mass: MIT Press, 2002), p.6.

42 Lucy Lippard, *Eva Hesse*, p. 160.

43 In Melissa Gregg and Gregory J. Seigworth (eds.) introduction to The Affect Theory Reader (Durham: Duke University Press, 2010) affectively titled, "An Inventory of Shimmers," descriptions range from "forces and resonances" and "persistent proof of a body's never less than ongoing immersion in and among the world's obstinacies and rhythms" (p. 1) to "a gradient of bodily capacity — a supple incrementalism of ever-modulating force-relations — that rises and falls not only along various rhythms and modalities of encounter but also through the troughs and sieves of sensation and sensibility, an incrementalism that coincides with belonging to comportments of matter of virtually any and every sort" with "immanent capacity for extending further still: both into and out of the interstices of the inorganic and non-living, the intracellular divulgences of sinew, tissue, and gut economies, and the vaporous evanescences of the incorporeal (events, atmospheres, feeling-tones)" (p. 2).

44 Sara Ahmed, *The Promise of Happiness* (Durham: Duke University Press, 2010), pp. 230–231.

45 Sara Ahmed, *The Cultural Politics of Emotion* (2nd ed.) (Edinburgh: Edinburgh University Press, 2014), p. 90.

46 Sara Ahmed, "Happy Objects," in *The Affect Theory Reader*,

p. 31.

47 Stephanie Weber, "Dynamic Topologies: On Consistency and Transience in the work of Senga Nengudi," in *Senga Nengudi: Topologies* (Munich: Hirmer Publishers, 2021), p. 37.

48 Oral history interview with Senga Nengudi, 2013 July 9–11. Available at https://www.aaa.si.edu/collections/interviews/oral-history-interview-senga-nengudi-16131

49 https://mcachicago.org/Publications/Websites/West-By-Midwest/Stories/Studio-Zs-Constellation

50 Senga Nengudi Performance Piece – Nylon Mesh and Maren Hassinger. Available at http://www.reactfeminism.org/entry.php?l=lb&id=258&e=t

51 Lovie Gyarkye, "An Artist's Continuing Exploration of the Human Form", *New York Times*, Nov. 9, 2020. Available at: https://www.nytimes.com/2020/11/09/t-magazine/senga-nengudi-art.html

52 Nengudi, Senga, Begum Yasar, Rizvana Bradley, Jessica Bell Brown, Ellen Y Tani, host institution Dominique Lévy, and host institution Dominique Lévy. Senga Nengudi. New York, N.Y: Dominique Lévy Gallery, 2015. p. 14.

53 ibid.

54 Natalie Hegert, "Respondez s'il vous plait: An Interview with Senga Nengudi," in *Mutual Art*, September 28, 2016. Available at https://www.mutualart.com/Article/Repondez-sil-vous- plait--An-Interview-wi/71B964571BB-7D4AF

55 Nengudi, Senga, Stefanie Weber, Matthias Mühling, host institution Städtische Galerie im Lenbachhaus München, host institution Museu de Arte de São Paulo Assis Chateaubriand, host institution Städtische Galerie im Lenbachhaus München, and host institution Museu de Arte de

São Paulo Assis Chateaubriand. Senga Nengudi : Topologien = Topologies. Edited by Stefanie Weber and Matthias Mühling (München: Hirmer, 2019), p. 51.

56 Bowles, John P., "Side by Side: Friendship as Critical Practice in the Performance Art of Senga Nengudi and Maren Hassinger," *Callaloo* 39, no. 2, 2016, p. 400.

57 *Topologies*, p. 51.

58 Louise K. Martell, "The Hospital and the Postpartum Experience: A Historical Analysis," *Journal of Obstetric, Gynecologic & Neonatal Nursing*, vol. 29, issue 1, 2000, p. 68.

59 Ibid.

60 Helen Marieskind, "The women's health movement," *International Journal of Health Services: Planning, Administration, Evaluation*, vol. 5,2, 1975, p. 218.

61 Smithsonian Institution Archives, Senga Nengudi papers, 1947, circa 1962-2017, Box 12, Folder 8: Photographs of Other Individuals, Locations, and Works of Art, circa 1962-1979, circa 1994, "Series: Photographic Material", Hospital photo order form.

62 Dorothy Roberts, *Killing the Black Body: Race Reproduction and the Meaning of Liberty* (New York: Pantheon Books, 1997), p. 89.

63 Ibid., p. 90.

64 Ibid.

65 Smithsonian Institution Archives, Oral History ID 16131, Audio excerpt: Oral history interview with Senga Nengudi, 2013 July 9-11, Available at: https://www.aaa.si.edu/collections/interviews/oral-history-interview-senga-nengudi-16131

66 *Topologies*, p. 46.

67 Ibid.

68 Elana Mann and Vera Brunner-Sung, "My Tribe: An Interview with Senga Nengudi," in *In the Canyon, Revise the*

Canon: Utopian Knowledge, Radical Pedagogy, and Artist-run Community Art Space in Southern California, edited by Géraldine Gourbe (Shelter Press, 2015).

69 Smithsonian Institution Archives, Oral History ID 16131, Audio excerpt: Oral history interview with Senga Nengudi, 2013 July 9-11, Available at: https://www.aaa.si.edu/collections/interviews/oral-history- interview-senga-nengudi-16131

70 Ibid.

71 Kellie Jones, "The World According to Z," in *Topologies*, p. 59.

72 Ibid.

73 *The Care Manifesto*, p. 16.

74 Joan Tronto, *Caring Democracy: Markets, Equality, Justice* (New York: New York University Press, 2013).

75 Griselda Pollock, *After-affects | after-images* (Manchester: Manchester University Press, 2013), pp. 201–201.

76 Ibid., pp. 207–208.

77 Alina Szapocznikow, *Sculpture Undone, 1955–1972* (New York; Brussels: Museum of Modern Art: Mercatorfonds, 2011), p. 28.

78 Carol Rama, *Antibodies* (New York: New Museum, 2017), p. 242.

79 Paul B. Preciado, "The Phantom Limb. Carol Rama and the History of Art," in *The Passion According to Carol Rama* (Barcelona: MACBA Museum of Contemporary Art of Barcelona, 2014), p. 16.

80 Sarah Lehrer-Graiwer, "A Carol Rama Panorama," in Carol Rama, *Antibodies*, p. 19.

81 Paul B. Preciado, "The Phantom Limb," p. 14.

82 Ibid., p. 23.

83 Ibid,.

84 Debbie Hillyerd, *Unconscious Landscape: Works from the Ursula Hauser Collection*, Exhibition Guide (Bruton: Hauser and Wirth, Somerset, 2019).

85 Eva Hesse, *Diaries*, p. 162.

86 Ibid., pp. 152–53

87 Ibid., pp. 152

88 Rebecca Kluchin, *Fit to Be Tied: Sterilization and Reproductive Rights in America, 1950–1980* (New Brunswick, NJ: Rutgers University Press, 2011), p. 1.

89 Kate Fisher, *Birth Control, Sex, and Marriage in Britain 1918–1960* (Oxford: Oxford University Press, 2006), p. 238.

90 Judith Orr, *Abortion Wars: The Fight for Reproductive Rights* (Bristol: University of Bristol, 2017), p. 3.

91 Alessandra Gribaldo, Maya D. Judd, and David I. Kertzer. "An Imperfect Contraceptive Society: Fertility and Contraception in Italy," *Population and Development Review* 35, no. 3, 2009, 555.

92 Rebecca Kluchin, *Fit to Be Tied*, p. 150.

93 Kate Pickert, *Radical: The Science, Culture, and History or Breast Cancer in America* (New York: Hatchette, 2019), p. 122.

94 Eva Hesse, *Diaries*, p. 651

95 Watkins, Elizabeth Siegel. *On the Pill : A Social History of Oral Contraceptives, 1950-1970* (Baltimore, Md. ; Johns Hopkins University Press, 1998), p. 38

96 Eva Hesse diary entry, January 1, 1967, Oberlin 1977.52.30, Eva Hesse Archive, Allen Memorial Art Museum, Oberlin College, Oberlin, Ohio; Eva Hesse papers, 1914–1970, bulk 1960–1970 dates. Archives of American Art, Smithsonian Institution.

97 Eva Hesse, *Diaries*, p. 604.

98 *The Care Manifesto,* p. 1.

Also available from Repeater

Justify My Love:

Sex, Subversion, & Music Video

by

Ryann Donnelly

In *Justify My Love*, Ryann Donnelly explores sex and gender in one of the most widely consumed art forms of our age — the music video.

Through an autobiographical reckoning with the author's life in a band and collaboration with past lovers, and a close analysis of the erotic iconography of music videos, *Justify My Love* tells the subversive history of this medium, from the inception of MTV in 1981 through to the 2010s.

Covering everything from Lady Gaga and Beyonce to Nine Inch Nails and George Michael, *Justify My Love* shows how subversion became mainstream, and how marginalised voices shaped some of the biggest music videos of the last thirty years.

Available from RepeaterBooks.com

REPEATER BOOKS

is dedicated to the creation of a new reality. The landscape of twenty-first-century arts and letters is faded and inert, riven by fashionable cynicism, egotistical self-reference and a nostalgia for the recent past. Repeater intends to add its voice to those movements that wish to enter history and assert control over its currents, gathering together scattered and isolated voices with those who have already called for an escape from Capitalist Realism. Our desire is to publish in every sphere and genre, combining vigorous dissent and a pragmatic willingness to succeed where messianic abstraction and quiescent co-option have stalled: abstention is not an option: we are alive and we don't agree.